BLOOMSBURY PUBLISHING, LONDON, NEW DELHI, NEW YORK AND SYDNEY

First published in Great Britain in September 2012
by Bloomsbury Publishing Plc
50 BEDFORD SQUARE, LONDON, WC1B 3DP
THE PIRATES! IN AN ADVENTURE WITH SCIENTISTS!™
RELEASED INTERNATIONALLY AS:
THE PIRATES! BAND OF MISFITS™
™ and © 2012 Sony Pictures Animation Inc.
Additional images courtesy of Shutterstock and iStockphoto

ALL RIGHTS RESERVED

No part of this publication may be reproduced or transmitted by any means, electronic, mechanical, photocopying or otherwise, without the prior permission of the publisher

A CIP catalogue record for this book is available from the British Library

ISBN 978 1 4088 2989 9 (HB)
ISBN 978 1 4088 3290 5 (PB)

PRINTED IN SLOVAKIA BY TBB, A.S.

1 3 5 7 9 10 8 6 4 2

All papers used by Bloomsbury Publishing are natural, recyclable products made from wood grown in well-managed forests. The manufacturing processes conform to the environmental regulations of the country of origin.

www.bloomsbury.com
www.thepirates-movie.co.uk

The Making of

With Questions and Answers by Hugh Grant

Written by Brian Sibley

BLOOMSBURY
LONDON · NEW DELHI · NEW YORK · SYDNEY

Welcome from Peter Lord

THINK OF ME as a doorman, or a butler if you prefer – maybe even Mister Bobo – standing at the entrance to this book in my smart suit. My job is to make a polite bow and say 'You're very welcome to the world of *The Pirates!* Make yourself at home. Stay as long as you like.'

As proud as I am of the film, I'm even more proud of the way it was made and of the people who made it. And so it's the greatest possible pleasure to be able to share some of the experience and the stories with you in this book.

What does the director of an animated film actually do? I've been asked it many times. Well, my job on *The Pirates!* was to have a vision for the movie and then to hold on to that vision, as firmly as possible over five years – during which time I had to make about a billion decisions (give or take a few). I had to have a view and make a choice on everything, from who to cast in the lead role, to the size of the buttons on Darwin's waistcoat.

Now five years sounds like a long time; and it would indeed be a marathon effort, if I wasn't supported every inch of the way and every second of the day by an astonishing team of uniquely skilled people – many of whom you'll meet in this book. At our studio in Bristol, we had all the skills to plan, design, build, light, shoot and animate this wonderfully rich, beautiful film – and then to go on to complete it with really special visual effects.

Hundreds of people were involved and – here's the great part – every one of them was better at his or her job than I would ever be. As a director, all I had to do was ask and someone could deliver exactly what I wanted, only better than I could have dreamt of. I can tell you it's a great feeling.

Now the first and most obvious thing to say about our style of film-making is that it's REAL. These days, we all know, everyone can make movies with astonishing computer effects. Animated movies and live action movies alike, they're full of brilliant images – huge armies, spaceships, monsters, explosions and death-defying stunts. We've all seen them. They're great. But here's the problem: they're not real. They're all made on a computer, and very well made they are too.

But our way of film-making is far more magical than that, because our world is handmade by the most skilled artists, craftsmen and animators you could ever find. You can see it on every page of this book: people working with hand and eye – building, painting, sculpting, drawing, animating – a brilliant mixture of genius and dedication. And THEN we add some of the most amazing and beautiful computer effects. It was a perfect combination of very different techniques, and it allowed me, as the director, to play in a bigger, better and more beautiful world than ever before.

But I shouldn't hold you up any more. Let me take your hats and coats. Welcome to our world. Have fun.

Contents

Welcome from Peter Lord
Questions and Answers by Hugh Grant

- CHAPTER 1 — A Cracking Good Yarn...Page 11
- CHAPTER 2 — Setting a Course for Adventure...Page 19
- CHAPTER 3 — The Pirates Awake...Page 33
- CHAPTER 4 — The Boldest Buccaneers...Page 39
- CHAPTER 5 — The Lubbers...Page 61
- CHAPTER 6 — Discovering New Lands...Page 75
- CHAPTER 7 — Pirate Paraphernalia...Page 99
- CHAPTER 8 — Avast! The Magic of Aardman...Page 107
- CHAPTER 9 — Baking Soda and a Beautiful Briny Sea...Page 125
- CHAPTER 10 — This Can Only End Brilliantly...Page 135

Questions & Answers

QUESTION 1:
How did you feel about being asked to work with Aardman and Sony on the Pirates film?

Pleased of course, but also suspicious and paranoid. I assumed Aardman had been leant on by the studio to hire a 'name' rather than continue to use the actor they'd used up to that point to make the superb rough (drawn) version of the film. Peter Lord denied my theory very charmingly for a bit, but I water boarded him and in the end he confessed that I was right. So while I was recording I was always paranoid that he was missing his first Pirate Captain. I'm sure he was. He probably still is.

QUESTION 2:
What was your take on the Pirate Captain as a character?

A poltroon of course – vain, inept, puffed up, a bit weak, but also innocent and endearing. I found all of those not impossible, although the innocent bit kept disappearing when I was recording and nervous. I was frankly marvellous in my kitchen at home. We should have recorded the film there.

QUESTION 3:
Are there any similarities between you and the Pirate Captain?

I do love to run people through.

QUESTION 4:
How did you prepare for the role? Did you eat lots of ham?

I went to Somalia and seized an oil tanker. I still have it.

QUESTION 5:
How did the recording process work with Aardman?

I would go into a dank dungeon in Soho, overact wildly for an hour, lose my voice, munch a lot of lozenges, overact some more and then trudge home feeling paranoid and queasy from the lozenges.

QUESTION 6:
How did it feel to see the Pirate Captain as an animated puppet?

Helpful. I found if I bulged my eyes in an endearing Aardman way and stroked a giant imaginary beard I was better. Later on I stroked Peter Lord's beard instead.

QUESTION 7:
How does this compare to live-action acting?

Aaarduous. And very poorly paid. But I calmed down after I realised that my puppet was compensating for my shortcomings. We gradually became close, as people do on film sets, and one thing led to another and now we're very happy and have just bought a cottage on Ham Common together.

QUESTION 8:
What interests you most about stop-frame animation? Were you surprised at the process?

I went to Bristol to meet the animators. They're mad. I wish I could find another word for them, but I can't. Six months to make 10 seconds of film. It was like having a nightmare about being made to play with your Action Man for ever and ever. And you're not even allowed to set him on fire at the end of it.

I
A Cracking Good Yarn

The inspiration for *The Pirates!*

A CRACKING GOOD YARN

It Started with a Story

> For Aardman, *The Pirates!* was a match made in heaven.
> – *Gavin Lines,* Supervising Graphic Designer

EVERY GREAT ANIMATED film from *The Pirates! In An Adventure with Scientists!* all the way back, seventy-five years, to the slightly shorter-titled *Snow White and the Seven Dwarfs* has one thing in common: a great story, strongly told.

Aardman Animations are past masters at storytelling, whether in the fleeting form of a TV commercial, a short film or a full-length feature. But finding a good story idea involves a lot of looking and a measure of good luck.

'Ideas are our lifeblood,' says Director Peter Lord, 'and because we are always looking for new ones, we have development meetings where people come along with books, scripts and comics and we look at whether there might be a way to develop them as future projects.'

At one such meeting, among some twenty books scattered on the table, was a copy of *The Pirates! In An Adventure With Scientists* by Gideon Defoe. 'My colleagues,' recalls Peter, 'thought it might make a possible television series, so I picked it up, started reading and was immediately hooked and laughing out loud. There was

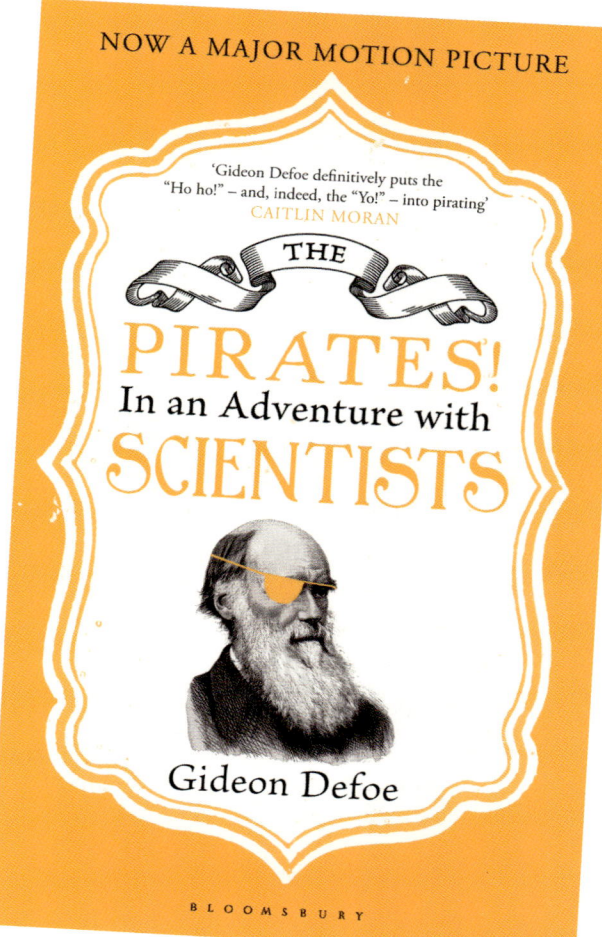

Above: the book that inspired the film

something spectacularly unique about it: a certain tone – comedy with a touch of surrealism, a love of absurdity and an intriguing use of language that was smart – very smart – and naive.'

Producer Julie Lockhart had a similar reaction: 'I was completely bowled over by the book and thought it the funniest thing I had read for a long, long time. It totally appealed to my sense of humour. Gideon has an original style of writing – silly and naughty – that makes you giggle. Any book that makes you giggle has got to be a good thing!'

Defining the book's appeal, Supervising Graphic Designer Gavin Lines says: 'I loved the anachronisms in the book: no worrying about historical accuracy, just whatever's funny.' For Editor Justin Krish, the novel succeeded in feeling fresh and new and, at the same time, very familiar. 'Most importantly,' he says, 'the characters are people with whom you want to spend time.'

And there were pirates! 'Obviously pirates were a big part of the appeal,' says Peter Lord, 'because the thing about pirates is they look so good! Real pirates probably weren't that great to be around, but these stories turned them into something glamorous, swaggering and colourful – pirate stories revel in the tropical seas, the blue skies, the cannons and costumes. It's a magical, irresistible world. So when we found this story about a crew of relentlessly optimistic pirates,

I felt we were telling a story in a sort of classic tradition, but turning everything up a notch.'

As Gideon Defoe sees it: 'Pirates are a group of people who go and have adventures for the sake of having adventures and that's a terrific route into a story. You don't need any set-up, you don't even have to do any research, especially if half the point is that the captain and his crew aren't very good at being pirates. They're pirates – of course they have adventures!'

Additionally, Gideon's distinctively quirky world had a very British sensibility that, as Peter immediately recognised, chimed with the already clearly defined Aardman sense of humour: 'There's a Britishness to our style of comedy – referencing all kinds of things from the Ealing film comedies of the 1940s and 50s to the cult 70s TV series *Monty Python's Flying Circus*. *The Pirates!* fitted that style perfectly.'

By the time he'd finished reading, Peter had reached a conclusion: 'The book had adventure, swashbuckling and comedy, but built everything together in a way I've never seen before. People approach a pirate yarn thinking they know what to expect and Gideon's story constantly undermines, exaggerates and plays with that expectation. It took but a moment to go from thinking that to saying: "This could be a film – let's give it a go!"'

CLOCKWISE FROM FAR LEFT:
Artist | All illustrations by Jonny Duddle

A CRACKING GOOD YARN

A Swashbuckling Adventure

'**IT'S ODD GOING** from writing books, where you have complete control and can spend all day in your pants and dressing gown, to a movie where absolutely everything is a huge collaboration and you have to turn up to meetings wearing proper clothes.' Gideon Defoe is talking about his transition from being author of *The Pirates! In An Adventure With Scientists* to screenwriter on the film.

The story actually begins, as Gideon explains, in 2003: 'Because of a daft bet with a friend and a misjudged attempt to impress a girl, I wrote a short, unremittingly stupid book about pirates. At the back of it, I added a joke "comprehension exercise" that included the question "Apart from Brian Blessed, who do you think should play the Pirate Captain if they were ever to make a movie of this book?" Obviously the joke is only funny because it's such a ludicrous question. Of course nobody would make a film of this book. It is, let's face it, unlikely enough that anybody would ever have published the

Facing page: author and screenwriter of *The Pirates!*, Gideon Defoe
Above: actor Brian Blessed with the puppet of his character, the Pirate King.

LEFT TO RIGHT:
Artist | All illustrations by Jonny Duddle

> Real piracy isn't about trophies! It's about fighting up staircases backwards! It's about sliding down sails with a knife in your teeth! Beard glossiness!
> —*The Pirate with a Scarf*

thing in the first place. Except now the book *has* been made into a film and, what's more, it even has Brian Blessed in it (though now promoted to Pirate King). As a result, the gag has been wrecked, the joke RUINED. Thanks a lot, Aardman!'

Unlikely though it may have seemed, the book found its way on to the desk of Peter Lord, co-founder of Aardman Animations. 'I later discovered,' says Gideon, 'that Pete has always had a bit of a soft spot for pirates, mainly so he'd have an excuse to dress up as one when it came to rehearsing the animation. But whatever his real motivation, he asked me down to Bristol to discuss the idea of turning it into a film.'

Like many of his generation, Gideon had grown up watching the animated antics of Peter Lord's famous modelling-clay character, Morph, and relishing the stop-motion animation that was a popular part of British children's television. 'As a kid, I think what's so appealing about stop-motion is that you can imagine doing it yourself, whereas I could never imagine drawing the hundreds of individual pictures that cel animation involves. Of course, once you see the level of complex work involved in stop-motion, you realise it's not quite as easy as it looks.'

The result of the meeting was, for Gideon, unexpected. 'Usually,' he says, 'somebody options your book, you sign away your rights, and then you have nothing to do with anything until you turn up at the premiere with your fingers crossed, desperately hoping they haven't totally screwed it up. To be honest, I'd have been quite happy with that, because if you were going to trust anybody to do a good job, it would be the guy that invented Morph! But what happened was something which pretty much never happens: Aardman were really keen for me to have a go at writing the screenplay, because they liked the tone of the book and thought I'd be the best person to try to keep that.'

Looking back, Gideon is grateful for how little he knew about the stop-motion animation process: 'I happily threw in big, exciting battles at sea, crowd scenes, costume changes and multiple locations, and gave characters luxuriant beards, because it never occurred to me that those things would create hugely difficult problems to overcome. Luckily, it was never a limitation. Nobody ever said, "We can't do this." It was always, "We'll work out a way." But the fact remains that if I'd had any frame of reference, I'd never have written it the way I wrote it and it would have probably ended up as two slugs sat in a room.'

A CRACKING GOOD YARN

Sony Climb Aboard

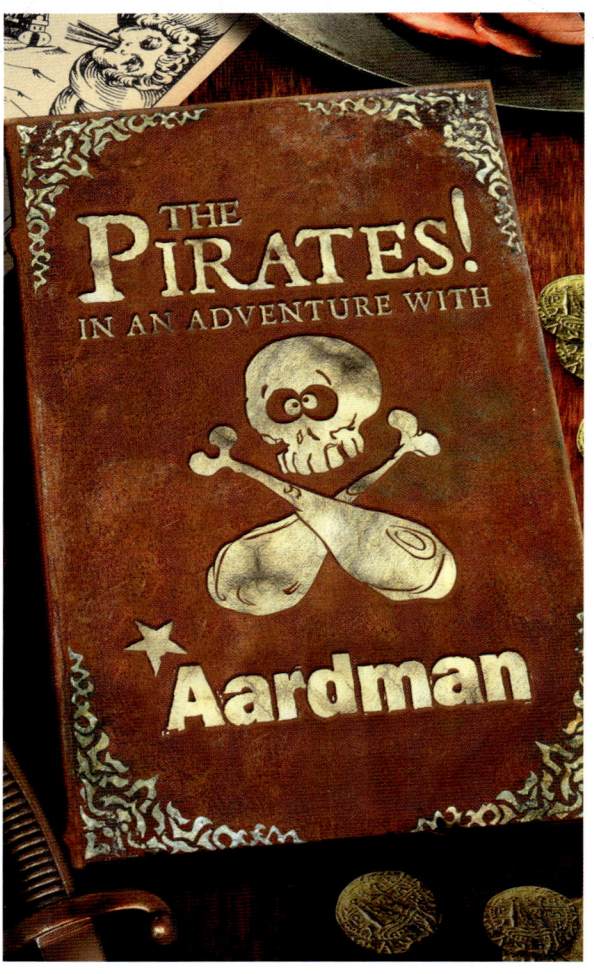

HAVING FALLEN FOR Gideon Defoe's zany sense of humour, Peter Lord and co-founder of Aardman, David Sproxton, decided to propose the idea to Sony Pictures Animation. 'We were in a new business and creative relationship with Sony,' says Peter, 'and, as they were very receptive to us, we decided to tell them about *The Pirates!* We hadn't had time to develop the idea, so we decided that our pitch would have to be a taster for what we wanted to do – a swashbuckling adventure told in a modern, slightly absurd voice.'

A short video presentation entitled *The Pirates! In An Adventure With Aardman* took the form of a wacky compilation of film and television clips giving oddball twists on historical events, accompanied by the highly piratical hornpipe music.

The presentation was well received by Michael Lynton, Chairman and CEO of Sony Pictures and Co-Chairman Amy Pascal, as Gideon Defoe recalls: 'At first there was a general assumption that this would probably have to be a strange little low-budget affair, because the book was quite odd, and didn't seem like the sort of thing you'd imagine a big Hollywood studio might go for. But when we pitched the idea to the Sony bosses, they were incredibly enthusiastic.'

'Animated films,' says Michael Lynton, who is also CEO of Sony Corporation of America, 'have a unique appeal that spans cultures and languages, making them an important component of Sony Pictures' global business. In Aardman, we recognised a creative partner with a widely respected style, and the ability to create highly original stories and some of the most memorable characters in animation today. Through our global production, marketing and distribution resources, we are proud to bring Aardman's captivating storytelling to the worldwide audience.'

'It's a thrilling partnership,' says David Sproxton. 'From the very beginning, when we first approached Sony Pictures Animation with the project, they were thrilled by this fun and unique take on the pirate movie, just as we were.'

A CRACKING GOOD YARN

The Pirates! set sail on a grand stage, ambitious for any medium, let alone the intricacy of stop-motion.
— *Hannah Minghella*

Nevertheless, as Producer Julie Lockhart readily admits, *The Pirates!* was unlike any stop-frame movie Aardman had ever made: 'It's so complex that the initial assumption was that we would do it as a computer-animated film. It wasn't until Peter decided that he wanted to build a set of the Captain's Cabin to use as a guide for the CG animators – to feel it and see the textures and really get that intricacy of it – we all decided it had to be done in stop-frame, even though it would be a tremendous challenge.'

Gideon Defoe and Peter Lord – aided by Sarah Smith and Peter Baynham, who had directed Aardman's *Arthur Christmas* for Sony, and the British screenwriting team of Andy Riley and Kevin Cecil – set about devising a treatment. A year later, they had a forty-page document outlining the story that was going to be told.

Sony's Hannah Minghella and Bob Osher, President of Sony Pictures Digital Productions, began regularly commuting between Los Angeles and Bristol. 'Generally speaking,' says Bob, 'our role was helping to shape the story, being very involved with the creative production and marketing teams at Sony, giving notes, thoughts and ideas. Basically I would say we were the fan club, being there to support the vision of Peter and the film-makers.'

'Peter Lord is a comedy genius,' says Hannah Minghella, now President of Production at Columbia Pictures. 'With a whimsical style, impeccable timing and brilliant characterisations, Peter's sense of humour and spirited storytelling established the Aardman sensibility from the start. One of the great joys in working with Peter and the Aardman team is to witness the sheer charm, delight and imagination with which these movies are made.'

Bob Osher agrees: 'The pace is slower, but the patience and artistry involved are astounding. What is especially interesting about Aardman's style is that there is a certain level of optimism and sweetness that transcends cultures. So does their physical sense of humour, which is unparalleled and plays universally.'

For Peter Lord, it was time to make his own personal commitment to *The Pirates!*: 'I always knew that I would direct it. I hadn't directed for a long time – having slipped into a development producer role – and thought if I didn't direct this film, I might never direct again. I was frightened because it is a gruelling job – lovely, but a bit of a life sentence. Nevertheless, I grabbed it! This was the moment and I made the choice. I said, "I think this is great and I'm having it!"'

Facing page: image specially created for Aardman's initial pitch to Sony Pictures Animation
Above: the Pirate Captain and his crew setting off in search of adventure.

II
Setting a Course for Adventure

Turning a daring idea into an even more daring screenplay

SETTING A COURSE FOR ADVENTURE

It's a Plunderful Life

HISTORICALLY, PIRATES MAY have been the terror of the high seas, but – regardless of their real-life exploits – it has been their destiny to become the stuff of romance and folklore.

Every age has celebrated the buccaneering life with imagination and inventiveness. In 1880, W.S. Gilbert and Arthur Sullivan wrote a comic opera, *The Pirates of Penzance*, featuring a character (without acknowledgement to the ruler of Blood Island) called the Pirate King.

The following year, the children's magazine *Young Folks* began serialising a tale entitled *Treasure Island, or The Mutiny of the Hispaniola*. Written by Robert Louis Stevenson, under the pen name 'Captain George North', *Treasure Island* was published as a book in 1883 and was the first pirate story to feature a map where X marks the spot for the buried gold. It also introduced the mutinous, one-legged sea-cook Long John Silver, with a parrot on his shoulder shrieking 'Pieces of Eight!'

Joining the Pirate Hall of Fame in 1904 was Captain James Hook when his ship, the *Jolly Roger*, dropped anchor off Never Land in

Above: N.C. Wyeth's 1911 illustrated edition of *Treasure Island*, published by Scribner

LEFT:
Artist | Jonny Duddle

J.M. Barrie's celebrated play *Peter Pan, or The Boy Who Wouldn't Grow Up*. According to the playwright, Hook was 'the only man Long John Silver ever feared'.

Hook and Silver were among a host of pirates whose careers received a boost with the coming of the movies – almost 150 of them – beginning with D.W. Griffith's 1908 silent film, *The Pirate's Gold*.

No less than thirty-five of these films appeared during the 1950s in a cinematic pirate-fest that included *The Crimson Pirate* with Burt Lancaster, *The Buccaneer* with Yul Brynner, *Against All Flags* with Errol Flynn and Walt Disney's *Treasure Island* in which Robert Newton gave a rip-roaring performance as Long John Silver that would remain the archetypal pirate image until, fifty years later, Captain Jack Sparrow pranced up the gang-plank of the *Black Pearl*.

Captain Jack brings us neatly back to Gideon Defoe's book. 'I was ahead of the curve,' says the author. '*The Pirates!* was written months before *Pirates of the Caribbean* made everybody love pirates, and years before *Pirates of the Caribbean 2*, *3* and *4* made everybody get a bit sick of them again.'

For director Peter Lord, Gideon's book brought back memories of the fun and games of those 1950s pirate pictures: 'The appeal was the joke of pirates as we imagine them. To make a joke you need to know your audience and you need to know the world you are referring to – and then find funny ways to do it. Gideon's pirates are not real pirates, but a childhood vision of pirates, derived from such films as *Treasure Island* and *The Crimson Pirate*: a comic interpretation of Hollywood inventions. I saw the visual potential at once: it pressed all the buttons.'

Classic pirate movie imagery: Robert Newton as the one-legged rascal, Long John Silver, menaces Jim Hawkins (Bobby Driscoll) in Walt Disney's 1950 version of *Treasure Island*. Photo: Ronald Grant Archive/Walt Disney Pictures

SETTING A COURSE FOR ADVENTURE

From Novel to Screenplay

'**How long does** it really take to write a story?' asks Director Peter Lord. The answer, it turns out, is over a year. *The Pirates!* began life in the pages of Gideon Defoe's book, but, as Peter explains: 'The story in the finished film is a complete re-think of the book. Everything, in the early days, was up for grabs.'

Reflecting on the process of dissection and reconstruction, Gideon says: 'Luckily, the book had only ever been what people call "a cult success", so there weren't vast legions of J.K.-Rowling-style fans to get angry if we messed with the story. We all agreed that we wanted to preserve the tone and certain elements of the story, but didn't necessarily want to be bound to the specific plot.'

Nevertheless, as Gideon admits, the process proved a steep learning curve: 'I discovered that it's much harder to write a movie than a book. Plot-wise, the book wanders all over the place, going

SQAUWK!

> We set a course at the start and kept on that course...
> —*Peter Lord*, Director

off on pointless tangents and not necessarily making much sense – and that's half the fun. But what works well in a book can make for a pretty unwatchable film. When you've only got ninety-odd minutes to tell your story, everything has to fit together in a precise way. Sometimes it ends up feeling more like doing maths than writing.'

Rejean Bourdages, heading up the film's story team, had the task of helping visualise a vision of the script: 'Our job is to collaborate with the writer and director in brainstorming and coming up with ideas and story solutions. We knew the book's humour would translate brilliantly; the difficulty was not letting the plot elements of the story overwhelm the innocence and fun of the characters. Luckily, Gideon wrote the script and was always around to make sure the characters stayed true to what he created.'

Producer Julie Lockhart reflects: 'We were

SETTING A COURSE FOR ADVENTURE

blessed that the script was extremely funny, right from the start – a very telling stage. After that, you just have to refine and refine.'

Gideon has his own idiosyncratic recollections of how those refinements were made: 'We all sat in a room and spent a seemingly never-ending amount of time writing things down on little yellow index cards, sticking them to the wall, moving them about and then throwing them in the bin before starting again with little blue index cards in the hope that changing colours might help us.'

The script went through five or six complete re-writes and there would be another twenty or so drafts during which elements, and even characters, were dropped or added. 'You always overestimate how much story you can get into the time,' says Peter Lord, 'so you always end up trimming back the story. For a long time the Pirate Captain was given a quest by a character called Calico Jack, who kept appearing in different forms in various scripts. There were so many versions of him – representing hundreds of hours of thinking and writing – but, eventually, that idea was completely lost.'

For several drafts there was a sequence featuring the Pirate Captain's stay in London after being pardoned by Queen Victoria. Becoming a celebrity and losing touch with his crew, the Captain was featured in magazines going to various social events, attending a show at the Royal Albert Hall and opening a donkey sanctuary.

Another lengthy scene (taken from the book) had the Pirate Captain tracking the Queen to her lair inside Big Ben. 'We had a very elaborate set-piece action sequence,' Peter recalls, 'taking place within the cogs of the clock. But this meant that we had one big showdown between the Pirate Captain and the Queen followed by another one – so one had to go. In each case you do all the work, fight for it, then ultimately lose it. It can be painful and, at the time, it always seems crucial.'

The challenge throughout was to keep the story focused on the central character of the Pirate Captain. 'Somehow,' says Gideon Defoe, 'the solution ended up being a dodo. I'm not quite sure how, but if you spend too long sitting in a room staring at index cards these things happen.'

Facing page and above: the 'lost character', Calico Jack, who in several early versions of the script provided the Pirate Captain with his 'mission'

LEFT TO RIGHT:
Artist | All illustrations by Jonny Duddle

SETTING A COURSE FOR ADVENTURE

Picturing the Story

Storyboard: the Blueprint for a Movie

'**THE FIRST EIGHTEEN** months is all about story.' Editor Justin Krish is talking about the difference between making a live-action feature film and an animated film. 'With live action, you shoot more than you can actually use. You shape the movie in editing and chuck away much more than you use. With an animated film, all the story editing happens at the beginning and it is done using the storyboard.'

Storyboards are a series of drawings representing each scene in the film with the dialogue spoken and specific details about how the camera will be used: a particular angle, a tracking shot, a close-up or a long-shot.

'Animation is such an expensive and time-consuming process,' says Head of Story Rejean Bourdages, 'that the storyboards allow the film-makers to see, at an early stage, what is working and what needs improving. It is an opportunity to iron out any kinks in the script and experiment

with ideas about sets, lighting and the way the characters will "act" before animation actually begins. It's the blueprint of your movie.'

Storyboarding was invented at the Walt Disney Studio in the early 1930s. Previously, Mickey Mouse cartoons had been planned using books of sketches, but by pinning those drawings on

SETTING A COURSE FOR ADVENTURE

> Here are the words of the script — now tell me that story in pictures.
> —*Peter Lord*, Director

to a bulletin board, it was possible to see the whole film from beginning to end at a glance and individual drawings could easily be moved, replaced or dropped. Other animation studios quickly adopted the system and within a decade it was also being used by some live-action filmmakers to plan complex action sequences.

In animation, the first storyboard is called the 'beat board': the bare bones of the story, visualised in around 3,000 images. Then the film is broken down into sequences and these are storyboarded in greater detail, adding gags and 'business' and indicating where a chase or an action sequence will be included, such as the bathtub roller-coaster episode in Darwin's house.

'The artist presents, or "pitches", the sequence to the director,' explains Rejean Bourdages, 'acting out all the roles and trying to get the scene to "play" as it will in the finished film. There will be notes from the director about what works and what doesn't and the storyboard will be revised – probably many times – before it is right. There's a lot of give and take and it's a constantly evolving process, but there's a saying in animation: "storyboarding is re-boarding".'

Justin Krish agrees: 'The storyboard is the fastest way to prototype new ideas and you carry on editing the storyboard right up to the end.'

The storyboard for *The Pirates!* finally featured over 55,000 images and, as Animation Supervisor Loyd Price points out, on such a complex production its importance cannot be overestimated: 'We had over forty units shooting scenes which meant that one shot might be animated by one unit and the next shot might not be filmed until six months later by another unit. The storyboard is the lynchpin that holds everything together.'

For Peter Lord, the storyboard is also an opportunity for everyone to contribute the kind of visual jokes for which Aardman are famous: 'As a director, I look to the story artists to come up with great jokes such as Rejean Bourdages having the idea for the sequence in the Royal Society, to play the theme from *2001: A Space Odyssey* on an accordion. Whether it's verbal comedy or visual comedy, there's nothing more satisfying than when someone takes a simple page of script and finds some moment that makes you laugh out loud!'

Facing page: helpful hints on where to locate images on a storyboard sketch! Director Peter Lord (sitting) discusses a section of the storyboard.
Right: the Pirate Captain comes aboard! Storyboard sketches by Dave Vinicombe

THE LOST SEQUENCE

'The only genuine research trip we ever did,' says Peter Lord, 'was for a chase sequence inside Big Ben with the Pirate Captain and Queen Victoria. We went up the clock tower at the Palace of Westminster, confidently expecting that we would be surrounded by the forty-foot-high cogs and gears we had imagined on our storyboards, only to find that the actual clock was the size of a small tea-chest.' Undaunted, the film-makers continued to develop the episode through at least three versions of the storyboard and had begun building a set when it was abandoned. 'We had one of those moments,' Peter recalls, 'that always occurs in making animated films, when someone says, "Hang on a minute – this is going to run to 110 minutes and we can't afford that!" That's when dramatic changes are made and on this film that meant Big Ben had to go.'

Above: Big Ben image by Well Done Films
Right: Big Ben storyboard sketches by David Vinicombe

27

SETTING A COURSE FOR ADVENTURE

The Bare Bones of a Blockbuster

'IT'S A BIT of a jack-of-all-trades job,' is how Head of Story Rejean Bourdages describes the task of storyboarding. 'In addition to being able to draw, the storyboard artist needs a basic knowledge of story structure, writing, cinematography, lighting and acting.'

The reason these skills are required is because the storyboard eventually becomes the story-reel: a filmed version of the thousands of storyboard sketches and, as Peter Lord explains, indications as to how the eventual animation will work: 'We include enough movement so that you always know what's happening. If, for example, the ship is sailing towards you, it will become progressively bigger in the sketches seen on screen; if a character gets cross, he will be represented by two drawings: one calm, one angry.'

Synchronised with a scratch soundtrack of voices, effects and music borrowed from other movies, the story-reel provides the director and his team with a first opportunity to see a projected version of the script and a chance to assess how the story will unfold on the screen. At the same time it highlights any amendments required by the storyboard prior to the start of animation. 'Story and pacing issues start to pop up,' says Rejean Bourdages, 'and it is at this point that the director and editor explore other options and sequences may be re-boarded until everyone is happy with the shape of the story.'

For the storyboard artist, the process means

having to accept that much of their work will go unacknowledged. 'Working on storyboards,' says Rejean Bourdages, 'means you are in on the ground floor of the film production. It's sad that, for many storyboarders, their actual drawings never make it into the final version of the film, but their ideas usually do, and you can see – albeit not literally – their fingerprints all over the screen.'

Producer Julie Lockhart describes the story-reel as 'the all-important heart of the film', but there is still one more important stage to be gone through before animation can begin. Called pre-visualisation (or pre-vis, for short) this is a version of the story-reel in computer-generated imagery (CGI) with very basic computerised figures and sets. 'What this allows us to do,' explains Peter Lord, 'is work out exactly what needs to be built for the studio floor and to pre-plan where the camera is going to be for scenes, what parts of the background and which characters will be in shot and, if there's to be a camera move – can it happen or will the camera bump into the set? Because time on the studio floor involves people, puppets and sets, it is very precious. Pre-vis enables us to avoid delays and be much more efficient in planning what we shoot and how we shoot it. But it's the craziest thing that we make the film three times: as a story-reel with filmed sketches; in pre-vis with rather clumsy CG figures; and then for a third and last time – for real – with the puppets!'

A vital component at the story-reel and pre-vis stages is the ability to be able to start thinking of the story not just in terms of pictures, but also sound. 'It's at this point,' says Peter, 'that we have to hear the words of the script – our characters now need voices.'

Facing page: the Pirate with the Accordion, and Peter Lord (left) recording 'piratey, bellow-rich' shanties by 'the legendary squeeze-box supremo', John Kirkpatrick.
Above: Jemma Lewis, editing

SETTING A COURSE FOR ADVENTURE

It's Only Impossible if You Stop to Think About It…

Hugh Grant (centre), voice of the Pirate Captain, on a visit to Aardman's studios, talks with Peter Lord (left) and Andrew Bloxham.

'THERE ARE ALWAYS awkward moments,' laughs Peter Lord, 'when, for example, you realise that you've asked Hugh Grant as the Pirate Captain to read the line "And?" in excess of forty times. That is a little embarrassing!'

As with every animated film, the voices are recorded before the animation begins. Initially, the story-reel had a vocal track featuring the film crew as the pirate crew, with Peter Lord as their Captain, but their enthusiastic performance was later replaced with a recording by professional actors and then – once the dialogue had been finalised – the roles were again passed on, this time to the stars.

Directing such notable names as Hugh Grant, Imelda Staunton, David Tennant and Brian Blessed was a man more experienced in getting Plasticine figures to do what he wants than in guiding the performances of famous actors. As Peter explains: 'This is a whole new, challenging side to directing. Most of the visual performance, the character and the emotion that comes across on screen, will be derived from the actor's voice. Getting an actor to understand the scene and then play it is a very two-way thing. You'd be a fool to go in and say, "This is what I want", because you want what an actor has to offer more than what you already have yourself!'

Peter gives an example of the many options that might be explored during a recording session: 'Let's choose a random line from the script… The Pirate Captain is going to say, "I've had enough of piracy, I'm hanging up my cutlass." How does he say that? He sounds pretty resigned, but is he really? Does he mean it? Is he fishing for a reaction? Is he self-dramatising in order to get sympathy? And if he does mean it, does he say it in a small defeated voice…? Or with a sigh? Or with forced cheerfulness, as if he thinks it's a good idea? Or as if he couldn't care less? The way the actor performs the line totally leads the way that the animator will perform it later.'

For Brian Blessed, playing the Pirate King, preparation was the key: 'I got to the studio

SETTING A COURSE FOR ADVENTURE

half an hour early and warmed up so that my adrenaline was high. Few actors could get the energy levels needed for someone like the Pirate King. He is a seething volcano, an atom bomb going off! I was determined that he would be the *crème de la crème*. Peter was very demanding and I could only get it right if I was superlative.'

It is a process that can leave the director feeling a bit at sea: 'You tend to end up sounding pretty stupid and uncertain,' says Peter. 'Just possibly an accurate picture. You find yourself saying: "OK, you're really furious in this scene, just let all the anger flow out!" Then, five minutes later: "OK, maybe the anger is all under control after all, you're suppressing it." And another five minutes on: "How about with a laugh in your voice, as if you're not really taking this too seriously." Finally, in desperation: "Could you do it in a high squeaky voice?" Or even: "Could you possibly sound a little more Swedish?"'

David Tennant provides the voice for Charles Darwin. 'My character,' he says, 'spends a fair amount of time getting hurt in a variety of comedic ways, so I've recorded a lot of panting and a lot of screaming! As actors we have to provide as many options as possible to give the animators the opportunity to play a scene in a variety of ways. We often do twenty takes so you have every conceivable reading of a line. The final decision on how this character will be played is taken in an animation studio far, far away; all I can do is, hopefully, provide whatever raw materials I can to make that character live as joyously as possible.'

Defining the relationship between director and actors, Peter Lord says: 'My job – apart from winding the actors up – is to make sure they know exactly the emotion and energy of the scene in question. Their job is to be lively, brilliant, funny, surprising, sincere – and everything else I ask of them! If you'll forgive a ridiculously contrived metaphor: they are the burst of elemental energy that makes the script suddenly spark into life, burst the leather straps holding it down, jump up off the operating table and then run off into the world outside, wreaking havoc!'

Above: actor Brian Blessed is introduced to the puppets.
Right: celebrated as being Doctor Who fans' all-time favourite Doctor, David Tennant gives voice and character to Charles Darwin.

III
The Pirates Awake

How a complete cast was designed
and modelled

Designing the Characters

'**AS A CHILD**,' recalls Jonny Duddle, 'I would constantly draw and always wanted to create characters and worlds. I loved books and animation and wanted to be either an artist or a Spitfire pilot when I was a grown-up.' As it happens Spitfire piloting lost out to art and Jonny is now an award-winning author and illustrator of children's books. He was also the character designer on *The Pirates!*

'In puppet animation,' says Peter Lord, 'every new puppet involves a huge amount of work and expense so you try not to make too many. On *The Curse of the Were-Rabbit* we had a total cast of about twenty and, for us, that was a lot. On *The Pirates!* we had an absurdly ambitious cast of characters – including vast numbers of extras that kept turning up: Napoleon, for example, is on screen for just twenty seconds!' And the former French emperor is just one of scores of characters (look out for

Charles Dickens, Jane Austen and the Elephant Man) giving cameo performances in the film.

While the storyboard was being developed, Peter, Co-Director Jeff Newitt and their colleagues were beginning to explore ideas about how the pirates and their world would be visualised on screen.

Flip through the pages of early character designs and you will find a treasure trove of inspirational concept art by a number of designers. There are paintings and drawings of pirates, queens, scientists and Londoners depicted in a variety of graphic styles from the look of classic book illustrations to rapid cartoony doodles. These ideas were gradually narrowed down to designs that not only capture the characters but also keep in mind that many moviegoers already have a very clear idea of what Aardman characters ought to look like!

Some characters went through many stages before their design was approved – in the case of the Pirate Captain, some fifteen to twenty different versions. Others, such as one of the first characters Jonny Duddle worked on, came to life very quickly.

'In the case of the Pirate with Prosthetics,' he says, 'Peter Lord described him to me as a particularly unlucky pirate so he wears an eye-patch, has a cork nose and is fitted with appendages made from an assortment of flotsam and jetsam including an antique chair leg! I started out with a very scrawly sheet of ideas from the practical (a "fishing rod attachment") to the downright silly (a "ship's biscuit ear"). I got lots of feedback, such as "wooden teeth are a great idea" and "I like his hook and the sort of wooden hinged arm that goes with it. No idea how it's meant to move, but somehow I don't think anybody's going to worry about that!" My concept works are just paintings and sketches; I don't really do anything differently to when I was a nine-year-old lying on my bedroom floor and drawing. True, designing characters for stop-motion animation brings new challenges, restrictions and considerations but there's also the opportunity to see those characters come to life.'

Indeed, once the directors had approved Jonny's designs, he made final detailed drawings, which the model-makers then turned into sculpted three-dimensional clay figures that would, eventually, become the basis for a cast of articulated puppets ready to step in front of a movie camera – and act!

... some of you are closer to being a chair or coat-rack than a pirate ...
– *The Pirate Captain*

Facing page:
Artist | Jonny Duddle
Artist | Warwick Johnson Cadwell
This page:
Artist | Jonny Duddle

THE PIRATES AWAKE

Making the Models

'**MODEL-MAKING IS** basically the same idea as casting in a live-action film,' says puppet designer Kate Anderson, one of the three creative heads – with Andrew Bloxham and Anne King – of Aardman's seventy-person puppet design team, responsible for transforming the character designs into the film's 112 three-dimensional puppet actors. 'We make the star, we make their wardrobe and their hair and we do their make-up. In a way, we're a lot of departments rolled into one.'

The process – a lengthy one that started a year ahead of filming – begins with what is called the 'sculpt': a clay sculpture that endeavours to capture the detail of the designer Jonny Duddle's drawings. 'The skill of being a sculptor,' says puppet designer Andrew Bloxham, 'is the interpretation of the drawing, and the initial sculpt is all about finding the character and vitality.'

For Andrew there is an excitement about sculpting a character for the first time: 'Sometimes you look at a drawing and instinctively know what the character is like. I couldn't wait to make Black Bellamy, because I could instantly see his personality. Sometimes it is more difficult: Darwin was very hard and went through many stages with several people having a go at sculpting his odd-shaped head!'

Once the sculpture is approved, a second version is made which divides the body up into the various elements – head, eyes, torso, arms, legs, hands and feet – that will be needed to build an articulated figure that can be animated.

These body parts are then moulded, painted and put back together to make the final working puppet. Or, in the case of the central characters, puppets, since no fewer than twenty Pirate Captains were built (with six costume changes) because, unlike human actors, Aardman's film stars are capable of shooting several different scenes on different sets at the same time.

However, like humans, the character puppets built with ball-and-socket joints so that they

Model-maker Josh Ashman selects mouths created through Rapid Prototyping from a mouth set.

THE PIRATES AWAKE

> All the pirate puppets are gorgeous. They're all standing around now waiting for their Big Moments on set.
>
> – *Peter Lord*, Director

can be animated. Film runs at a rate of twenty-four frames a second and the puppets are moved every other frame; so there are twelve moves per second, or 720 per minute.

One of the most difficult aspects of the animation – especially with 35cm-high puppets who will eventually be seen on the cinema screen enlarged to as much as twenty-five metres, is achieving convincing 'lip-sync': mouth movements that synchronise with the dialogue recorded by the voice actors. The speeches are given to an editor who breaks the lines down phonetically, so that if someone says, 'HELLO', that would be four mouth shapes ('Heh – l – uh – w') that will need to be animated.

Modelling and remodelling the mouth to match those sounds is incredibly time-consuming and on *The Pirates!* new technology called Rapid Prototyping came to the animators' aid, as RP Production Manager Jacky Priddle explains: 'Whereas we used to sculpt all of the individual mouth shapes (including teeth and tongues) out of Plasticine, we can now sculpt them using computer-generated imagery (CGI) then print them out in resin so that when cleaned up and painted (itself a highly intricate job) the mouths can be attached to the head of a puppet using magnets.'

Co-Director Jeff Newitt welcomes the innovation: 'It's really an ideal system, because the animators can concentrate on the performance and the characters' facial expression – they can get a wider range of movement because they're not worried about mucking up the modelling clay in the mouth shape.'

Almost 7,000 mouth shapes were made for the film's characters (at a rate of 100 a week) of which the Pirate Captain demanded as many as 1,400 solely for his own use. However, Queen Victoria's mouths proved the most time-consuming on account of the need to add Her Majesty's lipstick!

If mouths were challenging, beards were even more so. 'We had a lot of beards,' says Andrew Bloxham, 'including one for each of the twenty Pirate Captains, plus thirty replacements and five variants on his usual 'luxuriant' growth including one with bows and bling, a messy one with tufts, one that he could reach into (with rummage mechanism) and a special large version for the close-up of the fake Polly. Made in silicone, the hardest problem was to design a beard that would work with a very mobile and expressive face. We tried lots of different mechanisms using levers, joints, Allen keys and bits of wire before finally using a tuning head from a guitar.'

Above and facing: the Pirate Captain artwork in progress
Left: Will Harding sets up a hand armature in a mould prior to casting.

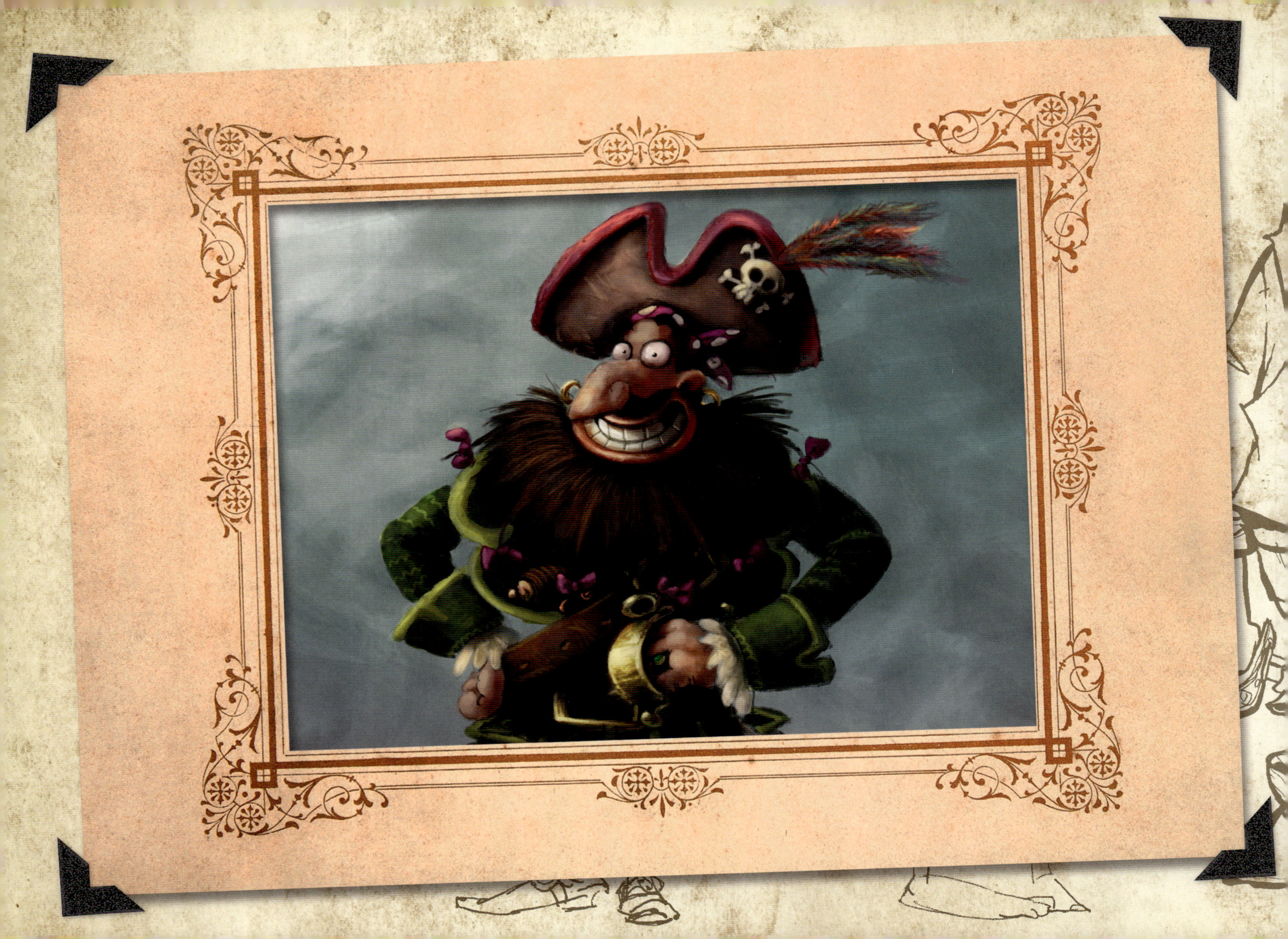

IV
The Boldest Buccaneers

The development and creation of the key pirate cast

The Pirate Captain

'**EYES GLITTERING, MAGNIFICENTLY** bearded, a face like thunder.' That is how the script dramatically describes the Pirate Captain's first appearance. But, as they say, appearances can be deceptive . . .

'He absolutely looks the part,' says Peter Lord, 'a big, beefy bloke who loves the job, the costume and everything about being the captain. But then Gideon Defoe turns this image on its head by making him self-centred, self-important and sensationally shallow with a total lack of concern for others. I think that's why everyone at Aardman sparked to this story – we love flawed characters who find a way to rise to the occasion in surprising, funny and clever ways.'

Above: early experiments with the Captain's design, both on the computer and in clay

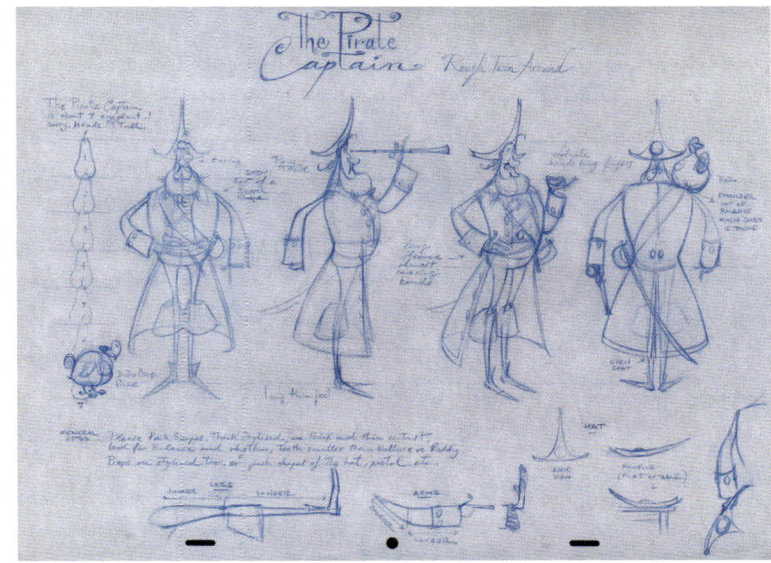

CLOCKWISE FROM FAR LEFT:

Artist | Jonny Duddle   Artist | Carlos Grangel
Artist | Carlos Grangel   Artist | Jonny Duddle
Artist | John Ogden   Artist | Warwick Johnson Cadwell

The truth is, as pirates, the Captain and his crew are amazingly incompetent. 'They're just rubbish at it!' says Hugh Grant, who provides the Pirate Captain's voice. 'They are really, really, really bad at piracy. But the Captain is perpetually optimistic, and because of that his crew is with him all the way. He loves his crew, he loves the ship's parrot – or, rather, what he thinks is the ship's parrot – and he is very vain about his luxuriant beard.'

Peter Lord points to other redeeming qualities: 'On the plus side, his vanity is so transparent as to be quite charming and he is useless at disguising what he is thinking, which gives him a kind of frankness. Essentially, he's a wholehearted character and unsinkably cheerful in a self-delusional way!'

However, he is still a spectacularly bad sailor, incapable of 'parking' his ship and seemingly unaware of the names of pieces of equipment, as when he gives the order: 'Fire those long things that go bang!'

> People to skewer.
> Places to pillage...
> Let's go plundering!
> – *The Pirate Captain*

LEFT TO RIGHT:
Early sketch – Peter Lord
Design for 'Pimped-up Captain' – Jonny Duddle
The finished puppet

> It's not all about me – no, no, no. Behind every Captain with glittering eyes and a luxuriant beard... there's a crew of briny rogues. — *The Pirate Captain*

There is a defining scene towards the end of the film where the Pirate Captain awkwardly admits to having let everybody down. But the Pirate with a Scarf will have none of it: 'You decided to single-handedly take on Queen Victoria's flagship in order to rescue Polly... That's terrifically idiotic! It's also the reason why me and the lads still think you're the best pirate on the seven seas.'

For Peter Lord, this is a moment that represents the theme of the film: 'It is about optimism, kindness and good humour winning out over the forces of cynicism and selfishness.'

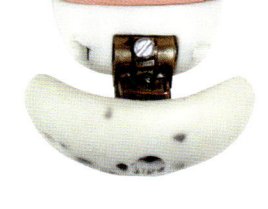

'The Captain is an idiot, but he's an idiot with a luxuriant beard,' says his creator, Gideon Defoe, adding: 'On the other hand, he is also boundlessly enthusiastic about everything. His great selling point is that he doesn't stop to think – he just jumps in. Of course, it usually ends up in disaster.'

Peter Lord also likes the Captain's enthusiasm: 'He is such a full-on, passionate pirate! He's like someone who plays football for a tiny, unglamorous club, but plays it body and soul. That and his cheerfulness are what win through – he's up against some very selfish and dangerous people, and there are not many things he can do better than they can, but his crew admire and respect him for being such a committed pirate.'

The Pirate Captain's luxuriant beard conceals a carefully engineered armature, accessed through a curl of hair. This enables it to be animated up and down, giving the beard a highly expressive life of its own.

Above left: the armature
Left: the face and beard armature in place
Below left: an early sketch showing the armature of the beard.

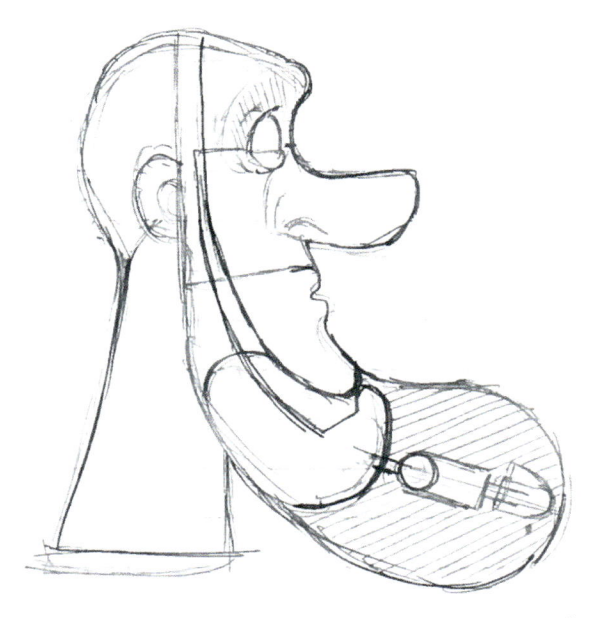

HANDS, KNEES AND...

Breaking the puppet body down into individual components enables the animators to adjust a figure's pose between frames. It also permits them to create movement and expression by changing parts, such as swapping closed hands for open ones. On the face, the animators shoot sequences using an array of different mouth shapes. This is finely judged to synchronise the character's speech ('lip-sync') with the vocal recordings of the actors.

I'd take a jellyfish in the face for that man.
— The Surprisingly Curvaceous Pirate

The Pirate Captain's head was not only complex in its design, it also presented a challenge for the Paint Department as the component pieces were made out of a variety of materials that needed to be precisely colour-matched. It was vital that the brow, head, and neck all featured an identical skin tone.

Hats
The Pirate Captain's main hat was fashioned out of resin, but other materials were employed for some scenes. A different, droopy sculpt was made when the hat was supposed to be wet, and a silicone one with a wire armature for when it needed to be animated.

Face parts
What with his luxuriant beard and hopeful smile, creating the Pirate Captain's head was always going to be a challenge! The head, mouth and beard parts were designed to lock together without moving, whilst at the same time allowing access for the mouth to be changed easily.

Moustache
The hand-painted foam moustaches had a simple wire armature which tended to snap as they were constantly being repositioned. When the production was at full pace, the crew made twenty a week.

Eyelids and eyebrows
While the Pirate Captain's eyebrows were created out of modelling clay and wax, the eyes were cast out of resin. It was an exacting process, requiring each eyeball to be turned on a lathe at different stages to set the iris in place. The eyelids were produced using the studio's innovative Rapid Prototyping technique. Each piece was so tiny, the animation crew constantly found themselves on hands and knees trying to find eyelids that had been accidently flicked on to the floor!

Mouths
The mouths were Rapid Prototyped from resin, but all painting was completed by hand. It required skill and a steady brush to colour up those tiny tongues and teeth!

Beard
The Pirate Captain's celebrated beard contained an armature accessed through a curl of hair permitting it to be animated up and down.

A typical mouth set created through Rapid Prototyping. The Pirate Captain has over 250 mouths.

45

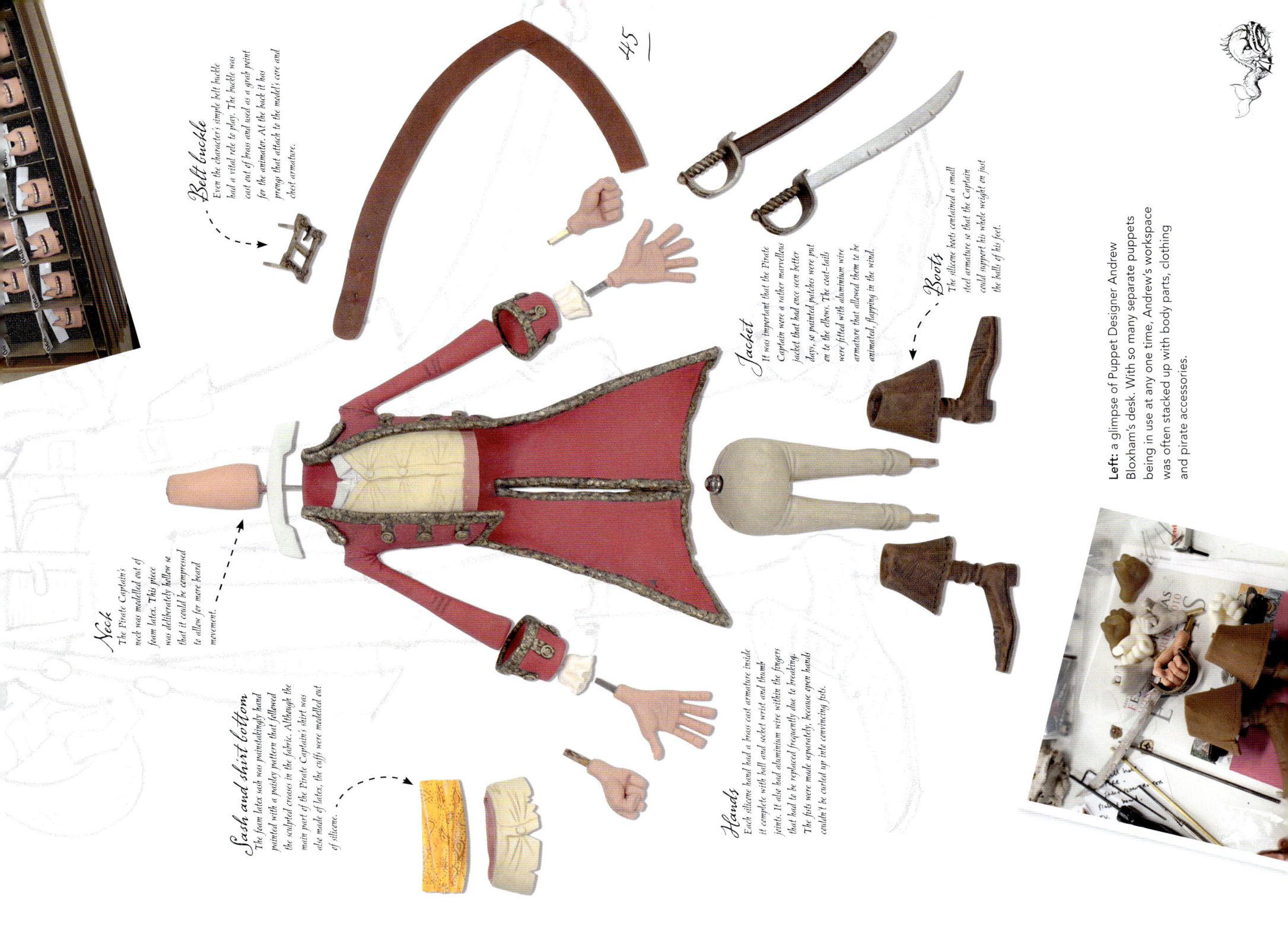

Belt buckle
Even the character's simple belt buckle had a vital role to play. The buckle was cast out of brass and used as a grab point for the animator. At the back it has a prong that attach to the model's core and chest armature.

Neck
The Pirate Captain's neck was modelled out of foam latex. This piece was deliberately hollow so that it could be compressed to allow for more beard movement.

Sash and shirt bottom
The foam latex sash was painstakingly hand painted with a paisley pattern that followed the sculpted creases in the fabric. Although the main part of the Pirate Captain's shirt was also made of latex, the cuffs were modelled out of silicone.

Hands
Each silicone hand had a brass cast armature inside it complete with ball and socket wrist and thumb joints. It also had aluminium wire within the fingers that had to be replaced frequently due to breaking. The fists were made separately, because open hands couldn't be curled up into convincing fists.

Jacket
It was important that the Pirate Captain wore a rather marvellous jacket that had once seen better days, so painted patches were put on to the elbows. The coat-tails were fitted with aluminium wire armature that allowed them to be animated, flapping in the wind.

Boots
The silicone boots contained a small steel armature so that the Captain could support his whole weight on just the balls of his feet.

Left: a glimpse of Puppet Designer Andrew Bloxham's desk. With so many separate puppets being in use at any one time, Andrew's workspace was often stacked up with body parts, clothing and pirate accessories.

The Pirate with a Scarf

'**HE'S THE VOICE** of reason,' says Gideon Defoe. 'The Pirate with a Scarf is kind of like Gromit to the Pirate Captain's Wallace.'

Martin Freeman, who provides Scarf's voice, agrees: 'There's a long tradition in British humour of someone who's cleverer than his superior. Scarf is just a bit more level-headed and unflappable. He keeps grounding the Pirate Captain: reminding him of his position, importance and responsibility to his crew.'

'Scarf is a really interesting and subtle character,' explains Peter Lord, 'because he genuinely likes and admires the Captain despite his many flaws. The fact that he remains totally devoted, whilst being completely aware that his boss is a liability, may seem illogical, but it has all the complexity and ambiguity of real life.'

'In a way,' says Martin Freeman, 'the Pirate with a Scarf is in the wrong job! None of the pirates are very good pirates, but they all clearly want to be pirates; it's the only role you can see them taking. But Scarf could be in middle management somewhere, or a solicitor perhaps. Instead, he's found himself on this ship – and he fits in quite well.'

> Captain, do you remember the little talk we had? The one about us trying to avoid hare-brained schemes that end in us facing certain death.
>
> – *The Pirate with a Scarf*

Facing Page:
The finished puppet
Character design – Jonny Duddle

This page, left to right:
Artist | John Ogden
Artist | Carlos Grangel

Below:
The puppet under construction

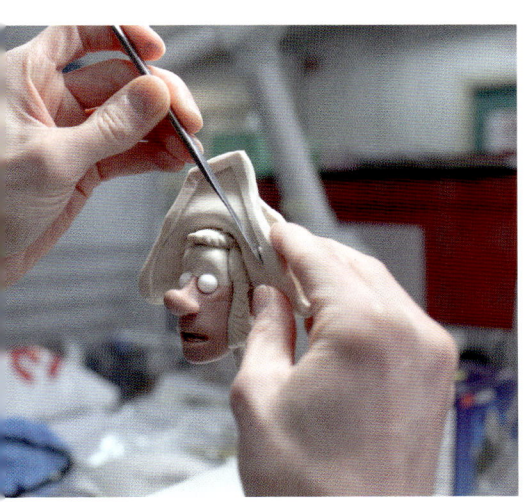

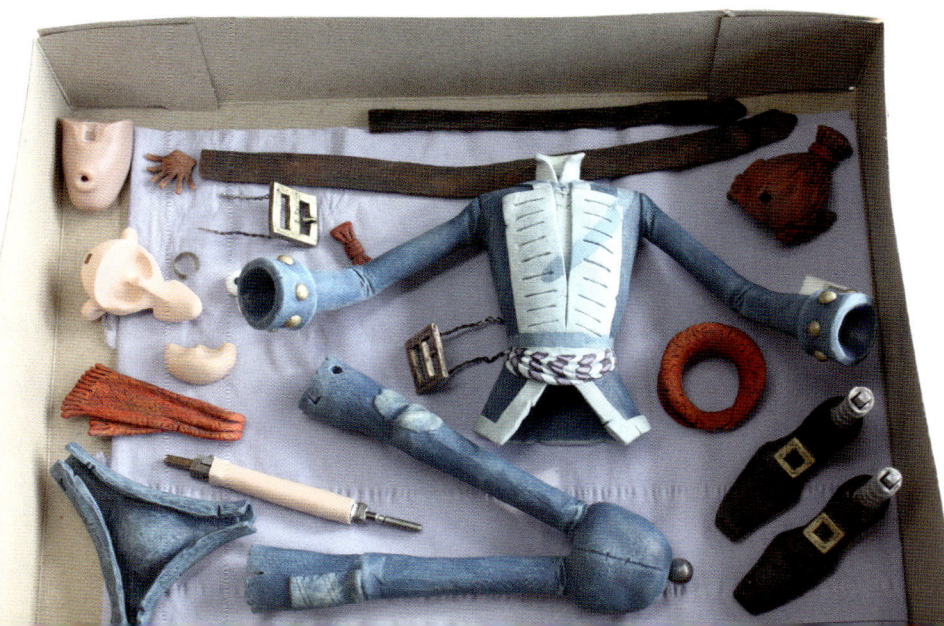

47

The Pirate with Gout

When the Pirate Captain, looking round his crew, says, 'Some of you are as ugly as a sea cucumber,' the Pirate with Gout doesn't take offence, he simply responds: 'Ah, get away with ya!'

Despite Gout's outward appearance of being a battle-scarred old sea dog, he's really just as daft and childlike as the rest of the crew. He is also singularly lacking in piratical bravado and when the Captain reminds everyone that they 'laugh in the face of danger', Gout is quick to say that *he* doesn't!

Most of the time, however, he is completely behind the Pirate Captain and even boldly declares: 'There's not a pirate on the seven seas can match you . . .' which is probably true!

LEFT TO RIGHT:
Colour design – Michael Salter
Design sculpt – Andrew Bloxham
The finished puppet

The Albino Pirate

The albino pirate
ZEBE's rough drawings, page#01

"**He is a** bit of a simpleton,' says actor Russell Tovey, who voices the Albino Pirate, 'but he's a loveable simpleton with a heart of gold.'

Somewhat excitable and nervous, Albino proudly announces that he has 'a badge for looting', but is also quick to admit: 'I don't really like danger at all.'

Innocent, gullible and naive, he has, as Peter Lord notes, a childlike knack for making the simple but revealing remark: 'When the crew are on Blood Island and see the booty taken by their rivals, Albino says, "Wow! We are rubbish compared to them, aren't we?" It's clearly never occurred to him before! They've been rubbish for twenty years, but suddenly he's had a revelation and cheerfully states the blindingly obvious!'

> *This can only end brilliantly!*
> — The Albino Pirate

CLOCKWISE FROM TOP:
Artist | Christophe 'Zebe' Lourdelet
Artist | Christophe 'Zebe' Lourdelet
The finished puppet
Artist | Michael Salter
Artist | Warwick Johnson Cadwell

The Surprisingly Curvaceous Pirate

ASHLEY JENSEN, WHO supplies the Surprisingly Curvaceous Pirate's unmanly voice, is puzzled: 'I'm not sure whether no one actually realises that she's female or whether they just don't mention it.'

Her true identity remains hidden behind a false beard that, as Peter Lord explains, provoked much discussion: 'This is a puppet film, so all the bearded characters have literally got stick-on beards! We had to find a different way of making hers actually look fake!'

The adoring expression on Curvaceous's face when looking at the Pirate Captain suggests that she doesn't exactly share the fraternal affection of the rest of the crew!

LEFT TO RIGHT:

Artist | Jonny Duddle
Artist | Christophe 'Zebe' Lourdelet
Artist | Christophe 'Zebe' Lourdelet
Artist | Michael Salter

Polly

'**POLLY.' SAYS PETER** Lord, 'was definitely not in the story at the start. Someone suggested the idea of a parrot that was actually a dodo, and from that point on the whole plot began to revolve around her.'

As she first appeared, Polly was given to the Pirate Captain by a character later dropped from the script, called Calico Jack. In that version, the Captain wasn't keen on what he thought of as just a big fat parrot. Only much later, when goaded by Black Bellamy, was he able to say: 'She's not fat, she's just big-boned.'

'I simply can't remember,' reflects Peter Lord, 'how we ever managed without Polly.'

In the final story, Polly became the feathery heart and soul of the boat, beloved by the entire crew.

LEFT TO RIGHT:
Artist | All illustrations by Jonny Duddle

Black Bellamy

OF ALL THE contenders for the Pirate of the Year Award, Black Bellamy is not only the most flamboyant but also the one most likely to win! 'He is provocative and irritating,' says Peter Lord, 'rather like an annoying neighbour who's always showing off because his house is better kept or he has a better car!'

He certainly gets under the Captain's skin when he mockingly asks: 'Did they change the rules? I mean, I always thought they gave it to the pirate with the most booty. Do they now just give it to the guy with the fattest parrot?'

Left: Jonny Duddle. **Above:** Peter Lord with Design Sculptor Debbie Smith and Black Bellamy

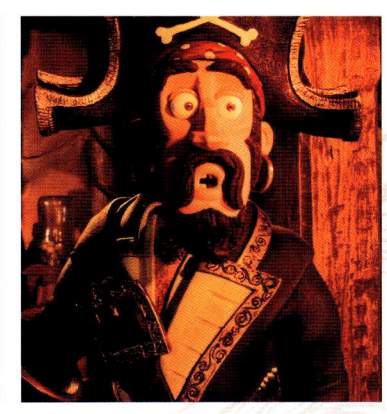

That's right! Black Bellamy is gonna be Pirate of the Year – again!

– *Black Bellamy*

BELOW, LEFT TO RIGHT:
Artist | Christophe 'Zebe' Lourdelet
Original design sculpt – Andrew Bloxham
The finished puppet

THE PIRATES! IN AN ADVENTURE WITH SCIENTISTS
BELLAMY rough drawings 01

53

Cutlass Liz

> Hello, boys! You're probably all wondering if I'm still as deadly as I am beautiful. Well, I *am*!

THE ONLY FEMALE contender for the Pirate of the Year Award, Cutlass Liz makes a dramatic entry into The Barnacle's Face tavern, blasting her way through the wall and striding through the rubble with a still-smoking cannon. 'It was a real hip-swaggering walk,' says animator Laurie Sitzia-Hammond, 'but with a swan-like demeanour in her upper body. I think she looks sassy!' Liz totes a huge diamond as her booty, but as the Pirate with a Scarf remarks: 'She doesn't even have a beard.'

Left to right: Michael Salter and Daniele Bigi; John Ogden; Jonny Duddle

Cutlass Liz

CLOCKWISE FROM LEFT:

Full colour design – Jonny Duddle
The finished puppet
Design sculpt – Ian Whitlock
Scale drawing – Jonny Duddle

55

Peg Leg Hastings

THE THIRD CONTENDER to rival the Pirate Captain for the Pirate of the Year Award is Peg Leg Hastings who, on his first appearance in The Barnacle's Face tavern on Blood Island, immediately trumps the Captain's paltry booty with a bulging bag of gold. The Pirate with a Scarf consoles the downcast Captain by remarking, 'Don't worry, sir. He's all flash and no bang!'

Pirate with Peg Leg

> Lock up your daughters! It's me! Peg Leg Hastings! Back from plundering the Spanish Main!
> *—Peg Leg Hastings*

Above: model-maker Lee Tetzner works on Peg Leg Hastings' dreadlocks.

ABOVE LEFT TO RIGHT:

Character design – John Ogden
The finished puppet
Character designs – Jonny Duddle

Right:
Design sculpt – Anne King

Far right:
Scale drawing – Jonny Duddle

57

The Pirate King

"**He is Blackbeard,** Long John Silver and Captain Flint all rolled into one!' Actor Brian Blessed is talking about providing the voice for the Pirate King.

'When he's very quiet, you have the sense that something is going to happen; then, suddenly, it's huge, it's a rush, it's all teeth! He's a very Shakespearean character. Wonderful! Powerful! One-eyed, ten feet tall and will knock anybody into next week! The most adored, respected and beloved of all the pirates, he is quite simply the best – bigger, braver, more ornate and exotic than everyone else. A giant of a guy in body, soul and mind, he is the definitive pirate and all roads lead to him.'

> Oh, villainous treachery! Treacherous villainy! You have betrayed the pirating fraternity!
> – *The Pirate King*

LEFT:

Artist | Jonny Duddle

59

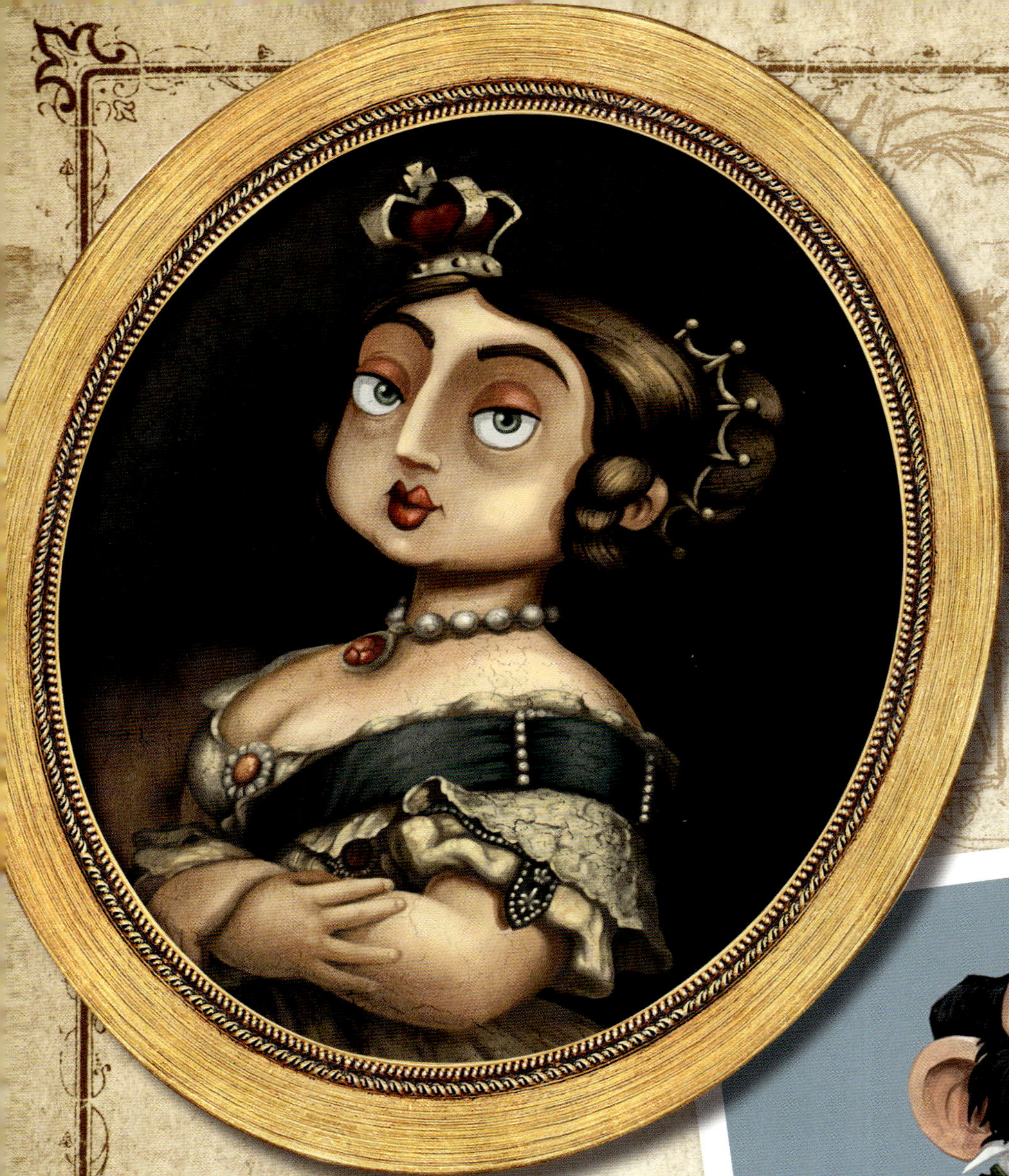

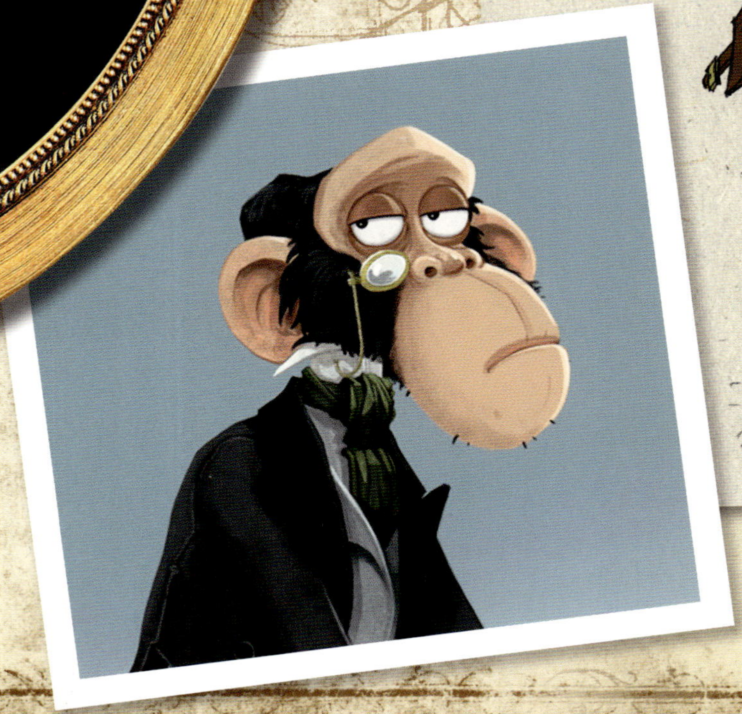

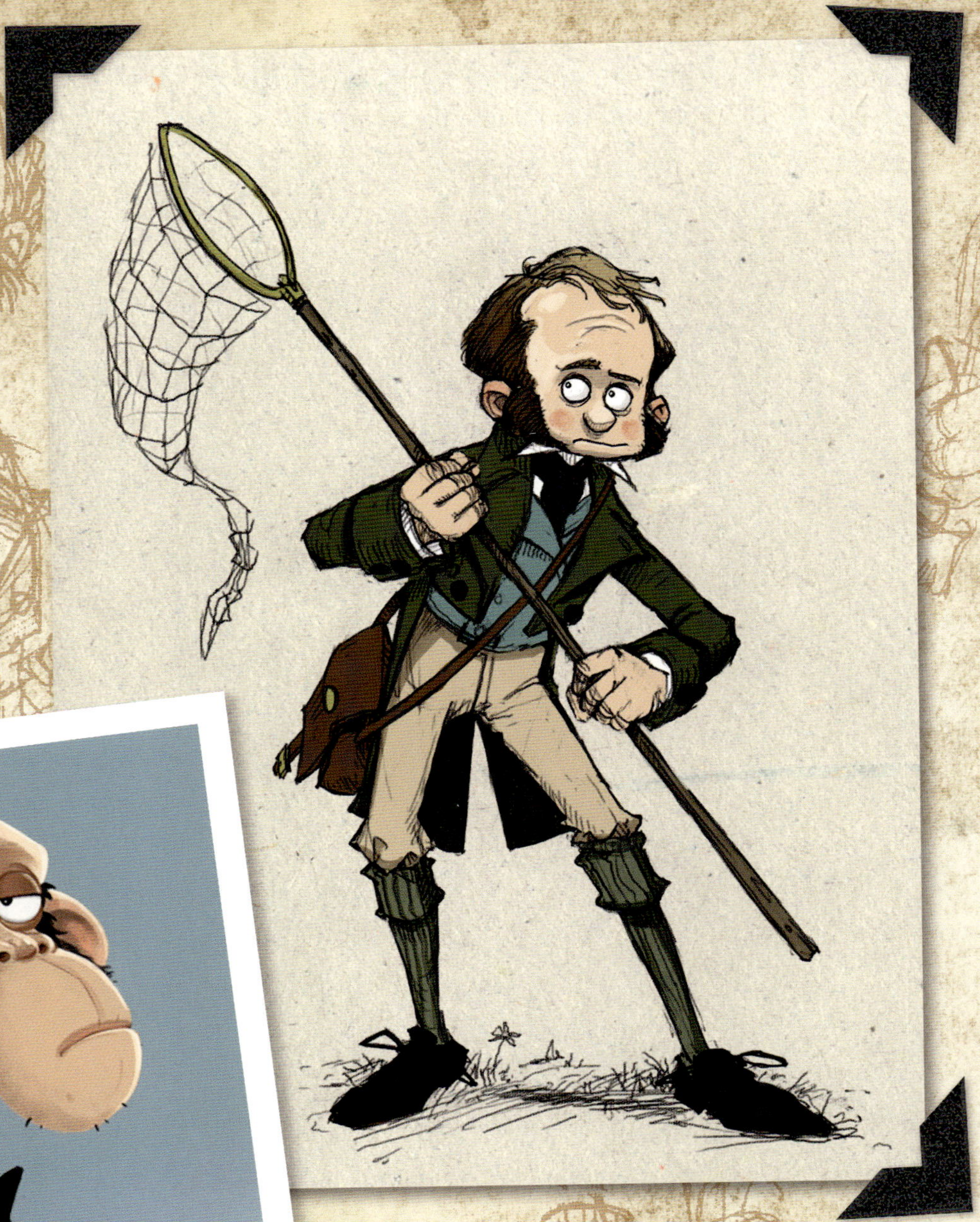

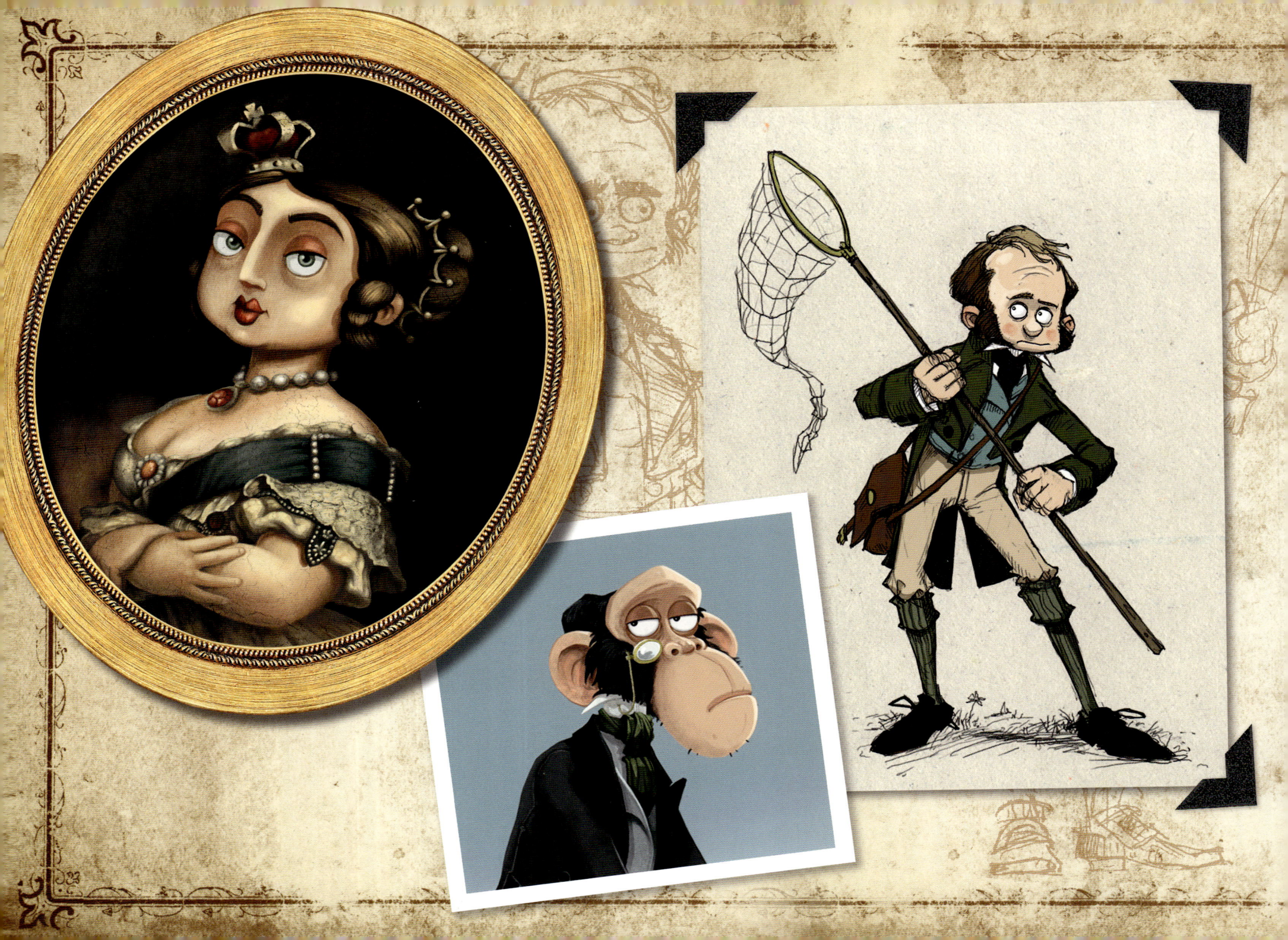

V
The Lubbers

Development and creation of the key Victorian cast

Darwin

'**I THINK IT'S TIME** to introduce another side of Charles Darwin to an expectant public,' says actor David Tennant, who provides his voice. 'This is a young Darwin, before he becomes world-famous, with terrible insecurities about his abilities as a scientist and as a man. He's rather smitten with Queen Victoria – his every motivation springs from his desire to impress her. I don't know if that's historically accurate – I'm just putting that out there – but his insecurities are what drive the plot in slightly unexpected directions.'

Character Designer Jonny Duddle recalls the process of deciding on Darwin's appearance: 'The idea was that he was a bit geeky, so we gave him a very big forehead. For inspiration, Peter Lord took some photos of himself posing in certain ways, including with a butterfly net, and I looked at Victorian references and portraits of Darwin himself. We'd continued to revise

CLOCKWISE FROM ABOVE:
Character sketches – Christophe 'Zebe' Lourdelet
Early designs – Jonny Duddle
Artist | Michael Salter and Daniele Bigi
Artist | Jonny Duddle
Colour design – Christophe 'Zebe' Lourdelet
Character sketches – Christophe 'Zebe' Lourdelet

63

> **I've managed to get Charles Darwin into a big-budget Hollywood animated movie, which seems kind of brilliantly unlikely.**
> – *Gideon Defoe*

the drawings – modifying how long his face was, how high his brow was, how old he seemed – trying to catch that Victorian egghead look.'

'I loved Darwin straight away,' says Ian Whitlock, the character's lead animator. 'You look at the drawings, read the script and start forming opinions about how the different characters might move and which of them you feel would best suit you as an animator. I liked the fact that Darwin had some great lines and a complex character, and then I heard David Tennant's vocal take on him and that really nailed it for me!'

'Darwin thinks he's cleverer than the Pirate Captain,' says David Tennant, 'and believes he can use the Captain for his own ends. It's a duplicitous relationship, but by the end they become rather fond of each other and they certainly have to work together in order to save the day.'

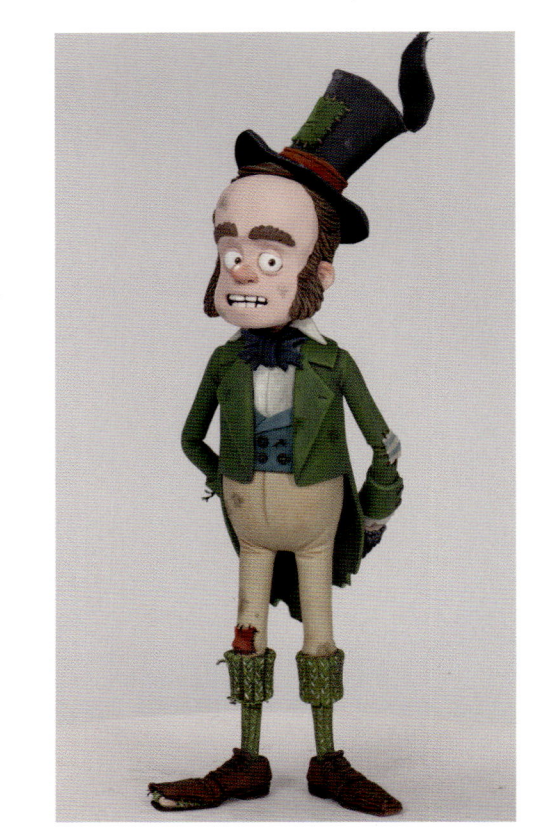

Looking back, author and screenwriter Gideon Defoe has vague qualms about how this famous historical figure is represented in the film: 'We have treated him with terrible disrespect. Apparently, he deserves a lot better than what we've done with him. But we've already made the movie, so there's nothing we can do about that now!'

CLOCKWISE FROM FAR LEFT:

Tramp design – Jonny Duddle
The finished puppet
Colour design over sculpt – Christophe 'Zebe' Lourdelet
Drawing – Jonny Duddle
Design sculpt with Polly – Andrew Bloxham

Mr Bobo

MR BOBO IS a joke that plays to the reader's general knowledge about Charles Darwin and the principles of evolution. In the film, the naturalist has come up with a theory, but it is, as Peter Lord puts it, 'an absurd travesty of what Darwin's theory actually was!'

'Don't mind Mister Bobo,' Darwin tells the pirates. 'Just an old project of mine. I had this theory. I thought that if you took a monkey, gave him a monocle and covered up his gigantic unsightly arse, then he would cease to be a monkey and become more of a Man-panzee, if you will.'

Although the Bobo experiment is a far cry from anything the real Charles Darwin ever had in mind,

Tea. Gentlemen?
– *Mr Bobo*

CLOCKWISE FROM RIGHT:
Colour design – Jonny Duddle
Design sketches – Jonny Duddle
Finished sculpt – Ian Whitlock

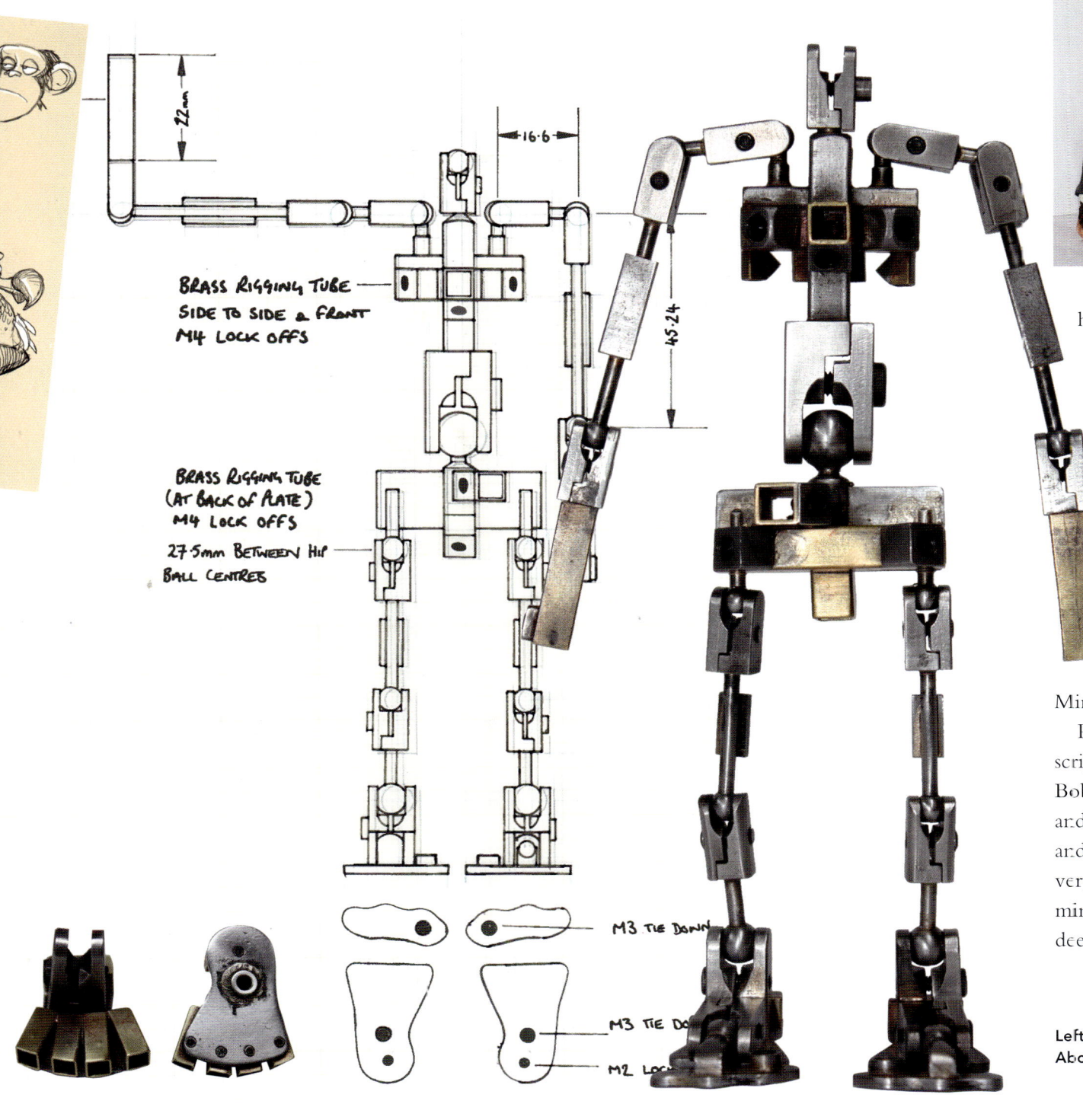

BRASS RIGGING TUBE SIDE TO SIDE & FRONT M4 LOCK OFFS

BRASS RIGGING TUBE (AT BACK OF PLATE) M4 LOCK OFFS

27.5mm BETWEEN HIP BALL CENTRES

M3 TIE DOWN

M3 TIE DO[WN]

M2 LOC[K]

he is a wonderful comic creation and – for a Man-panzee – plays an important role in the plan to save Polly. After that he, naturally, joins the pirate crew!

The gag, originating from Gideon Defoe's book, of Mr Bobo communicating through the use of flashcards (he seems to have every possible combination of words), provides many humorous moments in the film, as when the Pirate Captain asks, 'Are you with us, Mister Bobo?' and the reply, as he disappears, is a trail of flashcards reading: 'Are. You. Out. Of. Your. ★&^%ing. Mind.'

Peter Lord recalls a gag dropped from the final script: 'In one version we had a scene where Mister Bobo, having rowed across the sea to find the pirates and taken them to the *QVI*, whips out his flashcards and starts to tell them what is obviously a long and very complicated story; then we cut to twenty minutes later and the deck of the ship buried knee deep in flashcards!'

Left: Mr Bobo's armature and its working drawing – Jon Friar
Above: the finished puppet

Queen Victoria

> With their idiotic shanties and their ridiculous hats and their endless blasted roaring! I want them sunk. Scuppered. Smashed. Fed to the sharks! I HATE PIRATES!
> —*Queen Victoria*

JUDI DENCH, HELEN Mirren — eat your hearts out!' says Imelda Staunton, the latest actress to play a British monarch by providing the voice for Queen Victoria: 'It's fair to say this isn't a history lesson. Our Victoria has more than a couple of screws missing.'

As Peter Lord puts it: '*The Pirates!* is faithfully set in "the olden days" and that's about as accurate as it gets! Her Majesty wasn't in the book but in a story meeting it was decided that she would be the Pirate Captain's nemesis by threatening Polly. All the other crazy attributes just crept in . . .'

Opposite page:
Artist | All illustrations by Jonny Duddle

This page, clockwise:
Early design options – Jonny Duddle
The finished puppet
Production sculpt – Kate Anderson

69

As puppet designer Kate Anderson explains, Queen Victoria presented her own uniquely regal challenges when it came to building the puppet: 'On the outside she is quite a dumpy lady, but underneath, she has a complicated armature. All of the ruffles of her dress had to be made separately, so they could move around one on top of another. The torso had to be separate from the skirt and waistband so her body could be moved independently of the skirt, and the bustle could rise and fall to give her a look of walking.' Of the Queen's facial features, Kate says: 'She had to look pretty tough, royal and haughty, but wheedling and sweet as well. We pursed her lips to give her a disapproving look, but she is also the type of woman who can flutter her eyelids to get her way.'

Above right: Kate Anderson, model-making

Animator Suzy Parr says: 'the Queen was an extremely complicated model because of her skirt. Having been involved with her development, I then had to make sure the other animators knew her personality traits and how her armature worked.'

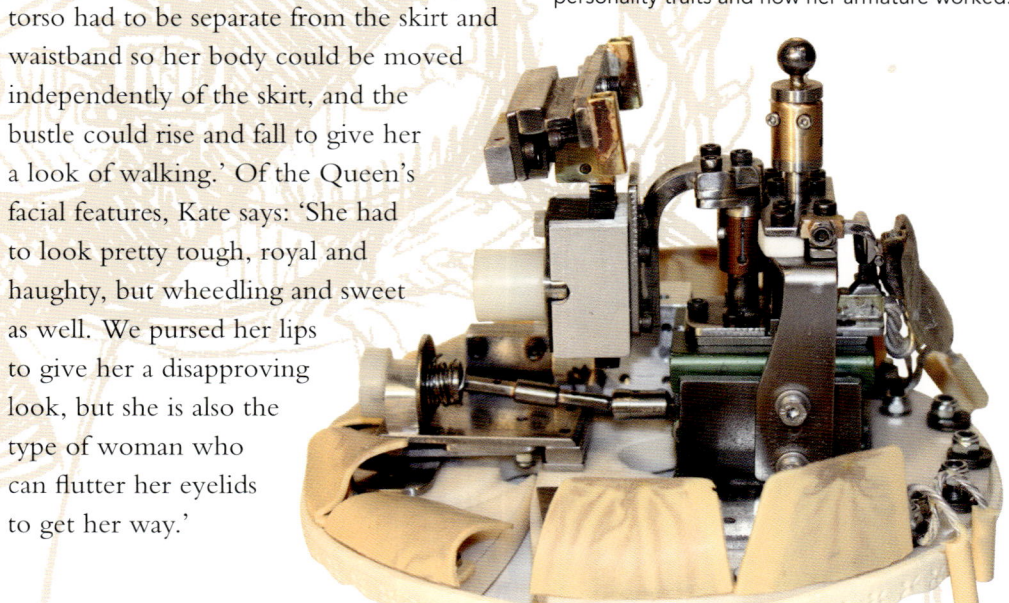

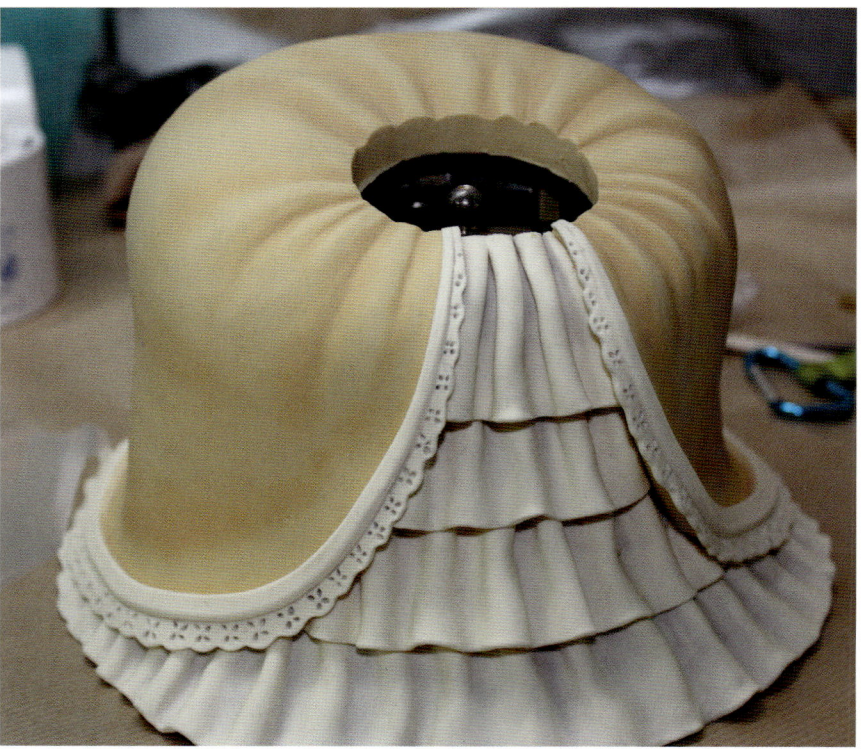

This page:
Drawings – Jonny Duddle
Design sculpts – Jay Grace

Suzy Parr helped develop Queen Victoria, using the early scratch voice recordings and doing tests to find out the limitations of the model: 'A lot of her character emerged once I had started shooting with her.'

'We based our Queen on the young Victoria,' says Peter Lord, 'taking the look and colour scheme from portraits of that period, and then threw everything at the concept with gay abandon. It's weirdly liberating to say "Never mind the history, we can do what we like!"'

Summing up her character, Imelda Staunton says: 'Poor Victoria – she does not like pirates, she wants a dodo, and she will do everything in her power to get one.'

The Supporting Cast

IN ADDITION TO the main puppet stars, there is a staggering supporting cast of 100 additional characters who may only have a line or two, or are simply extras glimpsed in the background.

There is the unfortunate Scarlet Morgan hanging in his cage on Execution Dock and additional members of the Pirate Captain's crew, such as the Pirate with an Accordion and a 'fish dressed up in a hat.'

There are also crowds of patrons in the taverns of Blood Island and London, plus scientists, Beefeaters, policemen, scientists, nudists, ghosts, scientists and street urchins – not to mention Queen Victoria's dinner guests from around the world and several historical figures, including aeronaut James Glaisher, physicist Michael Faraday, novelists Jane Austen and Charles Dickens, and the Elephant Man.

Much of the visual pleasure of *The Pirates!* comes from the supporting cast of minor characters and extras who are as detailed and rich in comic invention as the central players.

CLOCKWISE FROM FAR LEFT:

Artist | All illustrations by Jonny Duddle

Above: two of the Victorian age's most celebrated authors: Charles Dickens (left) and Jane Austen (centre) socialise with the Pirate Captain, Darwin and Mr Bobo.

73

SIDE ELEVATION

VI
Discovering New Lands

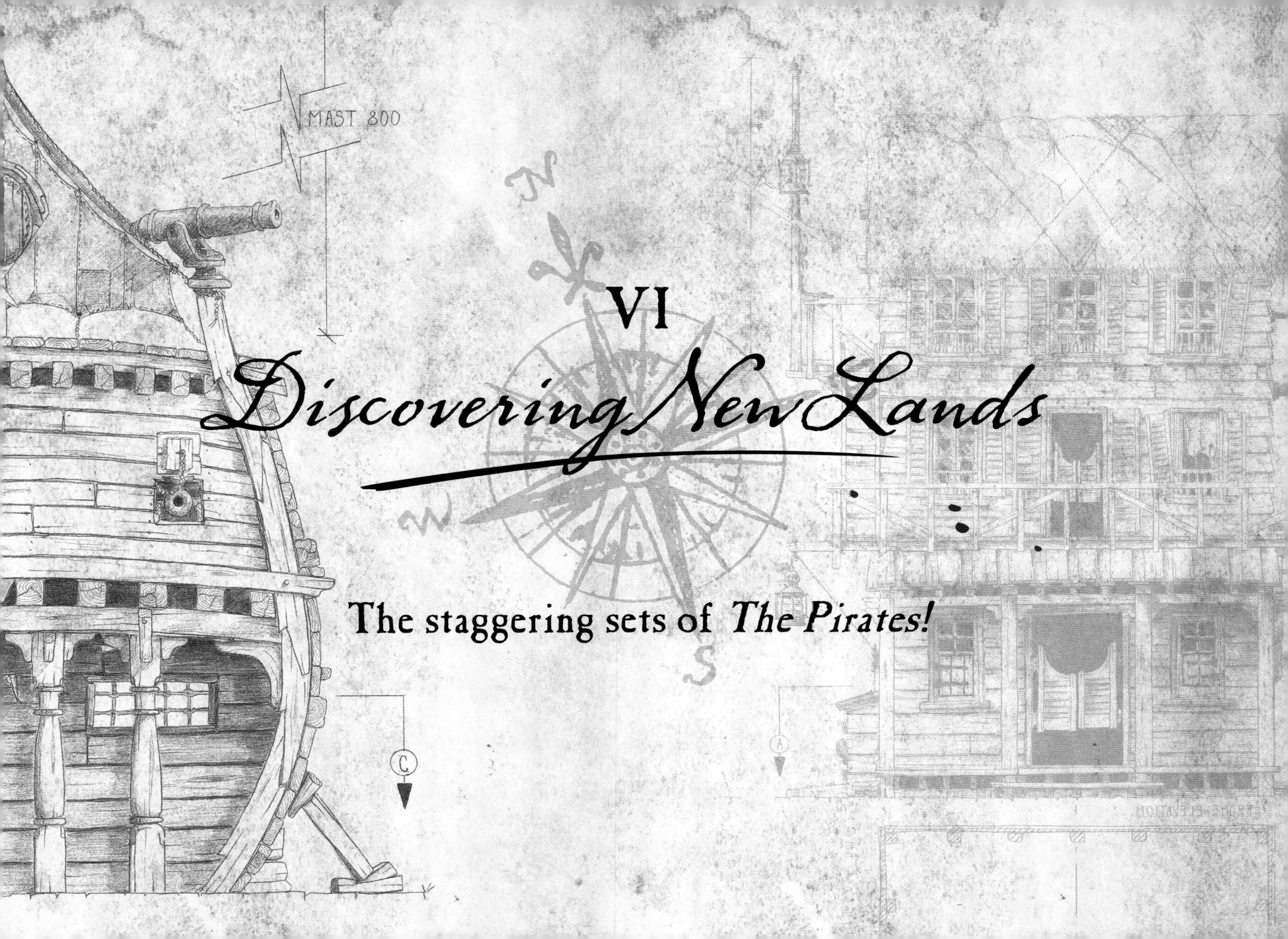

The staggering sets of *The Pirates!*

76

Bold Ambition

'**WE GO FROM** the pirate world to Victorian London, from the mean streets of the dockside to the Royal Society, the queen's dungeon and then back, again, to the high seas. Not one location gets repeated.' Producer Julie Lockhart is describing the diverse and immensely detailed sets created for the film.

The Production Designer responsible for creating the look for these locations was three-times Oscar®-nominee Norman Garwood: 'Peter Lord asked, "What does the Pirates' world look like?" My job was to try and provide an imaginative answer. He wanted a design that was funny and quirky. I was openly encouraged to be silly and daft and produce as many crazy-bonkers drawings as possible. My brief was extreme madness!'

Having previously designed pirate vessels for *The Princess Bride*, *Hook* and *Cutthroat Island*, Norman was given particular freedom when it came to the Pirate Captain's ship: 'I was allowed to go as wild as I could whilst ensuring that the ship looked real. Peter was adamant that it was not only what the pirates used for adventuring, it was where they lived – their home. It had to be fanciful, but believable.'

Eventually, the designs were translated into precise technical plans so that the set-builders could begin constructing the miniature but extraordinarily detailed environments for the characters to inhabit. In addition to believably conveying a sense of time and place, every set had to meet the very practical requirement of allowing the animators easy access to be able to reach and animate all the puppets.

Other sets had to be duplicated down to the tiniest detail so that more than one sequence could be shot in a particular location by different animators at the same time.

The pirate ship set presented its own unique challenges for which solutions needed to be found: from a complex arrangement of nylon threads attached to the sails and operated by motors to make them appear to billow in the wind; via heavy-duty mechanical gear and computer technology to enable the model to rise and fall with the ocean waves; to a quarter of a mile of rope for the ship's rigging that had to be unravelled, strengthened with wire and then glued back together again.

> This is my first animated film: the only difference is that the actors are twelve inches tall instead of six feet!
>
> —*Norman Garwood*, Production Designer

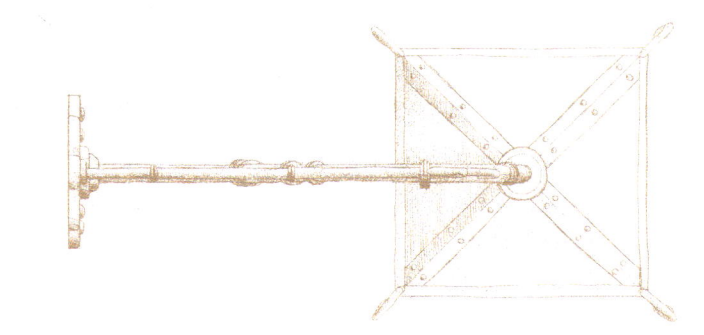

Facing page: Richard Hosken on set

The Ship

'**O**NCE UPON A time, in the olden days,' says Peter Lord, 'there was some crooked, backstreet boatyard that rather carelessly stuck two ships together. The front part was from 1820 and the back half from 1680 . . .'

The vessel is made up of two different boats. The back is what's left of the pirates' original funny old ship. In some terrible sea battle they lost the front and had it replaced with part of a once-elegant French frigate. Not being very successful pirates, they could never afford a new ship, so had to make do with one lashed together from bits and pieces and held together with chains and glue.

The ship has darned and patched sails, and mismatched rickety fixtures and fittings salvaged from other vessels. 'The ship has been badly maintained and has elements from all over the world,' says one of the film's art directors, Phil Lewis. 'There was a buxom figurehead that lost its head and was given a substitute head of Neptune (with painted-on lipstick); there are bits and pieces of chimney and the captain has a garden on the poop deck, where he keeps his collection of cactuses.'

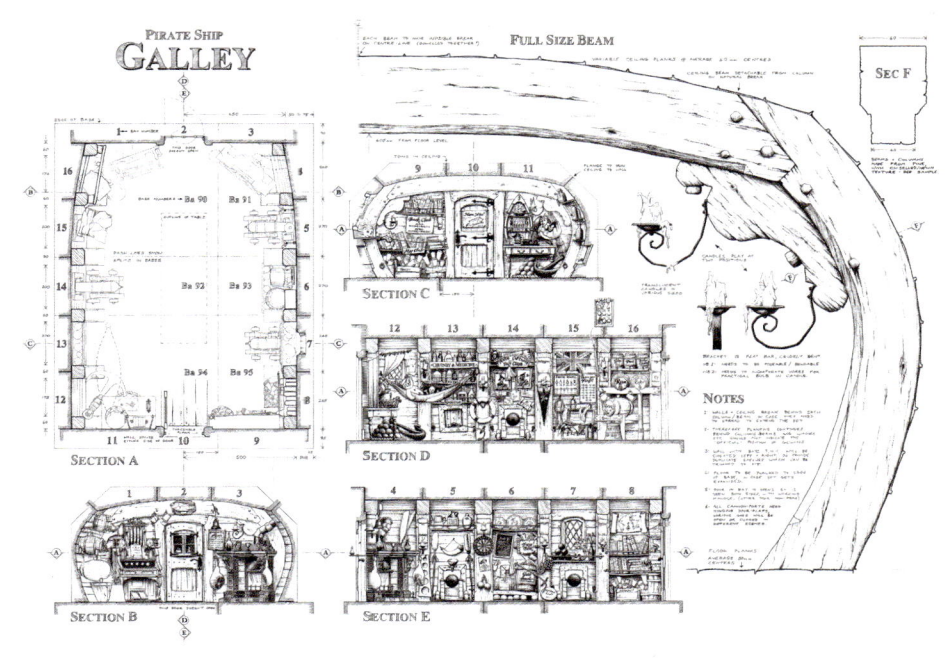

Once the design had been refined and finalised, a modelling clay mock-up of the ship was created and technical drawings were made so that the ship could be built as a physical stage to be acted on by the puppets. The massive set (4.25m long by 4.5m high) was also scanned into a computer so that a CGI (computer-generated imagery) version could be used for digitally created long-shots of the ship at sea.

One of the wackiest and most memorable cinematic ships was finally ready to set sail.

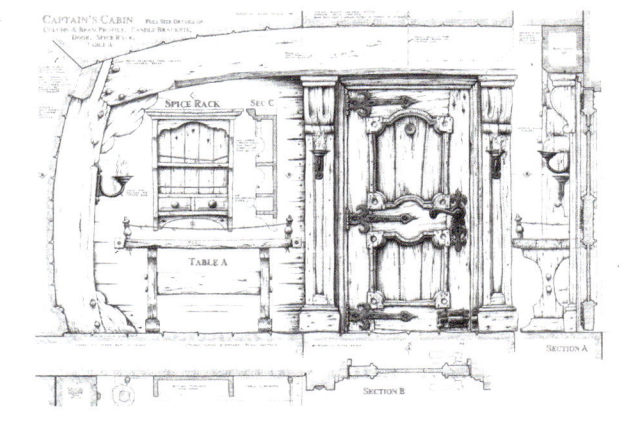

Facing page:
Ship design – Norman Garwood

Above and left: ship model and detailed working drawings by Phil Lewis

80

'I have designed a lot of pirate ships in my career, but as a concentrated bit of magic, this was the one for me!'

–*Norman Garwood*, Production Designer

Facing page: Richard Edmunds and Matt Perry on set
Above, right: Richard Haynes, animating

Blood Island

'**WE WANTED A** bit of madness,' is how Norman Garwood describes his concept designs for Blood Island, the heart and soul of piratical life on the seven seas.

The length of the waterside is crowded with a mishmash of buildings. Several dockside shops and taverns – including the palm-thatched Barnacle's Face Inn and Napoleon Blownapart's pirating supplies emporium – are made up of bits and pieces of salvaged wrecks. Elsewhere are shacks and shanties and a 'Jamaican Georgian' style house of the kind popular during the eighteenth century in Port Royal, Jamaica, then known as 'the wickedest city on earth' because it was a safe harbour for pirates and buccaneers.

Below: Norman Garwood's early designs and the finished look of Blood Islands
Bottom left: Matt Perry (left) and Norman Garwood with a scaled-down foam-core model of Blood Island

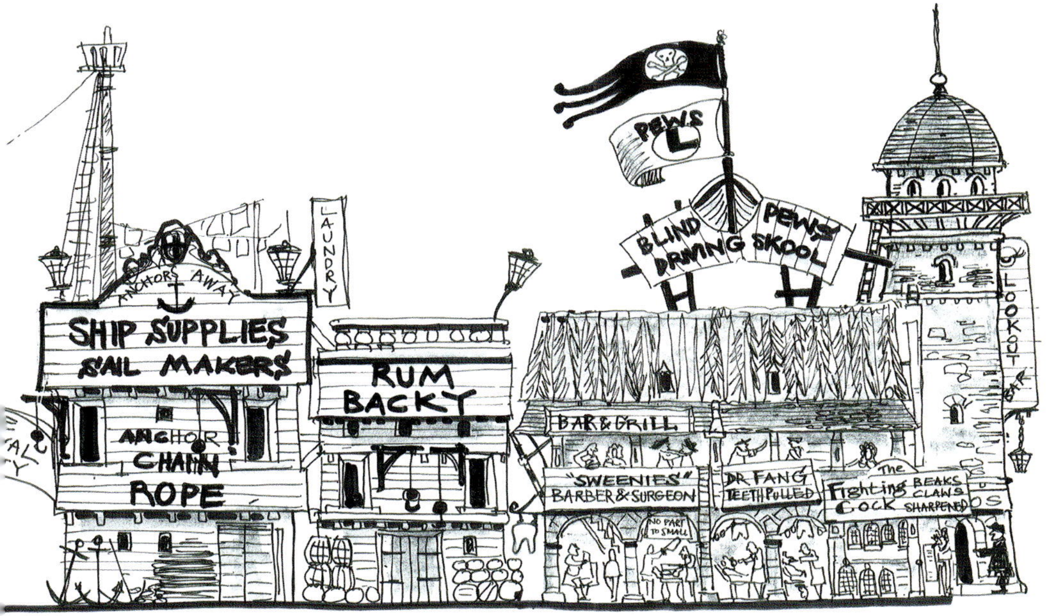
ANCHORS AWAY
SHIP SUPPLIES
SAIL MAKERS
ANCHOR
CHAIN
ROPE
LAUNDRY
RUM
BACKY
PEWS
L
BLIND PEWS DRIVING SKOOL
BAR & GRILL
"SWEENIES"
BARBER & SURGEON
DR FANG
TEETH PULLED
The Fighting Cock
BEAKS CLAWS SHARPENED
LOOKOUT BAR

BLIND PEWS DRIVING SCHOOL
SAUCY GIRLS
THE LOOKOUT BAR

The PIRATE of the YEAR AWARDS
AMPUTATIONS
HOP ALONG HAWKINS
MAST RAISERS & SHIP SUPPLIES
GANGPLANKS
BIGGEST EVER SAIL
BLIND PEWS DRIVING SCHOOL
GRINDHOUSE
BEAUTIFUL GIRLS for DANCING OR ROMANCING
HELLO SAILOR
WORLD of HAM
TATTOOS
LOOKOUT BAR

The crowded dockside is framed by palm trees and set against a backdrop of rolling, wooded hills leading up to a great volcano. 'We love having everything built in the studio,' says Peter Lord, 'but Blood Island was so enormous, we simply couldn't do that, so everything you see behind the quayside buildings was created by the film's computer graphics team.'

One regret for Peter is the fact that most of the fantastic detail in the set goes unnoticed: 'I would love to have spent more time on the harbour front with the crew stopping to look in shop windows. But the pace of the story wouldn't let me linger! I just had to settle for Blood Island making a spectacular if all too brief appearance.'

Far left: Malcolm Lamont, animating
Below: Andy Brown and Stuart Mallaber, set dressing. Blood Island was shot against a green-screen background. The distant mountains, palm trees and the ocean were all added later as Special FX.

85

Victorian London

'**LONDON HAD TO** be London,' says Production Designer Norman Garwood, 'but over the top!' Nevertheless, the designs began with extensive research into the Victorian period, with one particular book helping to define the visual mood. *London: A Pilgrimage*, published in 1872, portrayed the city in 180 sombre, intensely detailed engravings by the French illustrator Gustave Doré. 'I loved using Doré's book,' says Norman Garwood, 'because he authentically captured every aspect of the place and time – London: posh and poor.'

The film-makers also considered earlier screen representations of London, viewing classic black-and-white films such as *Gaslight* and various movie versions of Dickens' novels and the Sherlock Holmes stories. As Norman explains: 'The design brief was for London to be a scary place – even for pirates – so that if you went down any of the dark, fog-filled alleyways, Jack the Ripper might well be lurking there.'

Above: the influence of the art of Gustave Doré on Norman Garwood's designs can be seen from Doré's 1872 engraving, 'Ludgate Hill: A Block in the Street'.

NB: PLEASE RETAIN WONKINESS, AS INDICATED

TERRA COTTA RIDGE TILES

WONKY BLUE-GREY SLATES, WITH LICHEN + MOSS, ETC

FOR FULL-SIZE GUTTERS AND DRAINPIPE DETAILS, SEE BLD 04/01

Ⓐ SEE SIGN DETAIL BELOW RIGHT

FOR LAMP DETAIL SEE P/H 371
ALL LAMPS PRACTICAL

Ⓑ
NB= GLAZING SLIGHTLY TEXTURED, SO WE CAN SEE LIGHTS + SHADOWS INSIDE, WITHOUT SEEING THROUGH TOO CLEARLY.

Ⓒ

Two-Faced Fool — Turncoat Ales

1,000 mm

Left and above: the 'Two-Faced Fool' tavern (purveyors of Turncoat Ales) eventually became 'The Hook Line & Sinker', where the Pirate Captain is taken by Darwin and Mr Bobo.

87

London smells like Grandma.
— The Albino Pirate

Supervising Art Director Matt Perry adds: 'We wanted Victorian London to feel scuzzy, dank and rich in its textures and in creating the sets, we tilted some of the buildings to make them seem more intimidating. A sign on one of the walls sums up the feel: "Sewage delivered to your door"!'

'Essentially,' says Norman Garwood, 'the London in *The Pirates!* is what people imagine Victorian London used to look like in their psyche.'

Right: Alison Evans, animating
Facing page: Loyd Price, animating

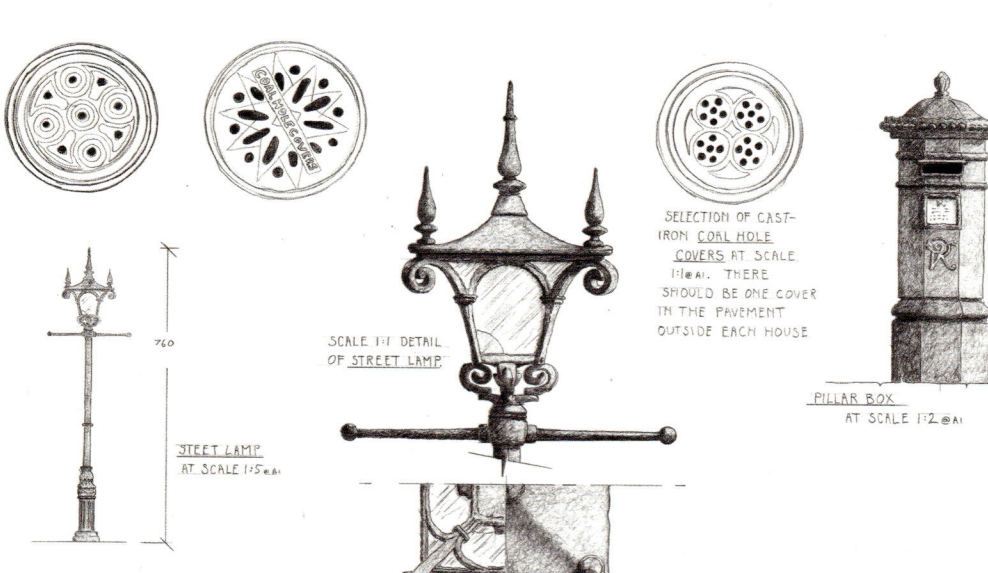

ROYAL SOCIETY
CIENTIST of the YEAR
SCIENTISTS ONLY
BEYOND THIS POINT
LONDON TAXI CABS

Darwin's Cabin

DARWIN'S WORLD OF science is immediately established in his first scene. Seated at his desk, surrounded by research, in a cabin crowded with bones and specimens floating in jars, he is busy writing . . .

'Journal of Charles Darwin. Day ninety-three aboard the *Beagle*. I have today discovered a new kind of barnacle, which I have categorised in the order of Pygophora . . .'

He pauses, stares at a large portrait of Queen Victoria, sighs and continues: 'I'll never get a girlfriend. I am so unhappy.' That's when a cannonball smashes through the wall and hits Her Majesty in the face. '. . . And now I'm being attacked by pirates!'

The Pirate Captain:
No gold, eh? Then what, might I ask, is this?!

Darwin:
It's a baboon's kidney.

This page:
Artist | All illustrations by Jonny Duddle

Darwin's House

ON ARRIVING AT Darwin's London home, the Albino Pirate anxiously remarks: 'People who live alone are always serial killers'. Indeed, the first thing to say about the place is that it looks more like the home of the Addams family.

'It's an American Gothic vision of architecture,' says Peter Lord, 'and it's absolutely wrong for London but its wrongness is funny! Everything about the place amuses me. When we first meet Darwin on the *Beagle*, he seems a rather pathetic, not very successful, little man; yet he somehow maintains an enormous mansion in London

— there's no logic to it whatsoever!'

Appropriately for the man who pioneered a theory of evolution, Darwin's house 'evolved', as Peter explains: 'Most people know that Charles Darwin was a naturalist, but his film house is a cross between that of a big-game hunter and a museum. The walls are covered in animal-head trophies and there are masses of exhibits, including a dinosaur skeleton and an Easter Island statue – not to mention a ridiculously large stuffed elephant up near the top of the house, which is most impractical! The fact is, most of the things are either there as gags or because we needed them for the crazy bobsled-style chase sequence in the bathtub!'

CLOCKWISE FROM FAR LEFT:
Drawings – Jonny Duddle
Animal heads and small props – Diego Soriano Gomez

The QV1

'THERE WAS A kind of logic behind the creation of the *QV1* – or at least a train of thought.' Peter Lord is discussing Queen Victoria's royal flagship. 'One of the themes was that the pirates live in the past and the modern industrial world has no room for the romantic nonsense of piracy. So, we decided to contrast the captain's wonderfully quirky, homemade, wooden ship with a great iron dreadnought of a vessel belonging to Her Majesty.'

One of the visual inspirations for the *QV1* was the SS *Great Britain*, designed by Isambard Kingdom Brunel and launched in 1843. The largest ship afloat at the time, she was the first iron steamer to cross the Atlantic. Built in Bristol, the SS *Great Britain* is now a tourist attraction in Bristol Docks, not far from the Aardman studios.

As the design developed, it was decided that the *QV1* required a rather more spectacular appearance than that of any authentic historical vessel, as Peter explains: 'The iron-hulled steamships of the Victorian era don't have much in the way of flair or swagger about them and, frankly, they looked rather dull and boring up against the Pirate Captain's craft. That led us to the wild fantasy of topping off the *QV1* with the Indian-inspired domes of the Royal Pavilion in Brighton.'

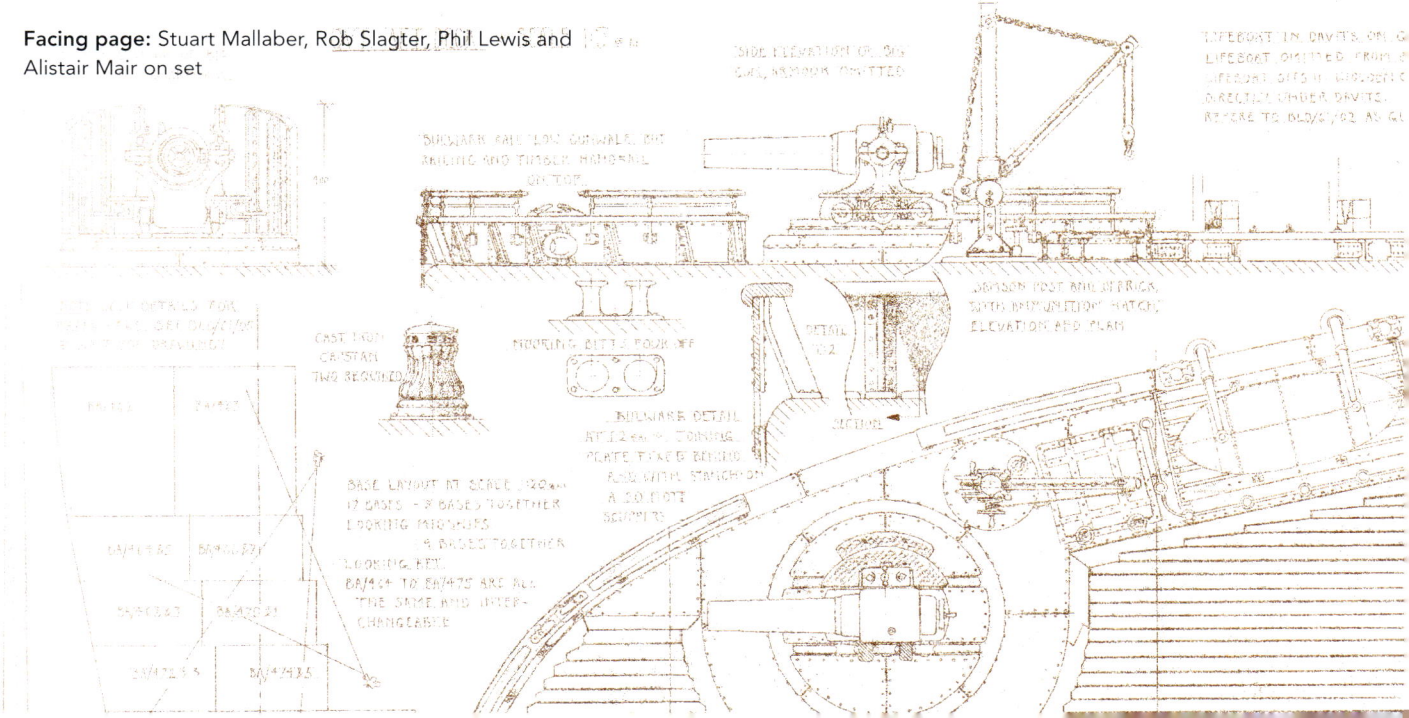

Facing page: Stuart Mallaber, Rob Slagter, Phil Lewis and Alistair Mair on set

The Prince Regent's extravagant nineteenth-century royal residence also had an impact on the interiors of the *QV1*, with its elaborate kitchen and a banqueting room which has echoes of the Royal Pavilion's colour scheme and detailing – especially the use of chinoiserie, a French term for a European style of decorative architecture that is Chinese-esque.

Above: Rhodri Lovett, animating
Below: Small props for the kitchen – Diego Soriano Gomez

Above: one of the kitchen sets. The art department needed to make six different sets, looking at the kitchen from several directions. Thousands of small props were created, including pots and pans, vegetables and exotic animals – many of them already cooked.

"BRINY ROGUES" ~ INT. Q.V. DINING ROOM ~ BALCONY BALUSTRADE ~ SCALE

NOTE: BALUSTRADE HANDED DOWN CENTRE LINE

BALCONY HANDRAIL CURVED TO FOLLOW LINE OF ROOM

Above: guests at Queen Victoria's Rare Creatures Dining Club Annual Banquet for World Leaders include a Spanish Queen and a Zulu Chief (left), a helmeted German and (right) Napoleon and Uncle Sam!

F.S. SECTION THROUGH (A)(A)

TRUE SIDE ELEVATION OF BALCONY BEAM

What kind of ship is this?
— *The Pirate Captain*

WANTED
PIRATE CAPTAIN

12 DOUBLOONS REWARD

*AND A FREE PEN!

VII
Pirate Paraphernalia

Signs, charts and pirate kit

HAM

NAPOLEON BLOWNAPART

'HOP-ALONG' HAWKINS
BESPOKE CRUTCHES • WOODEN LEGS

PRETTY POLLY'S Parrot-Phernalia
FOR ALL YOUR PSITTACINAE NEEDS

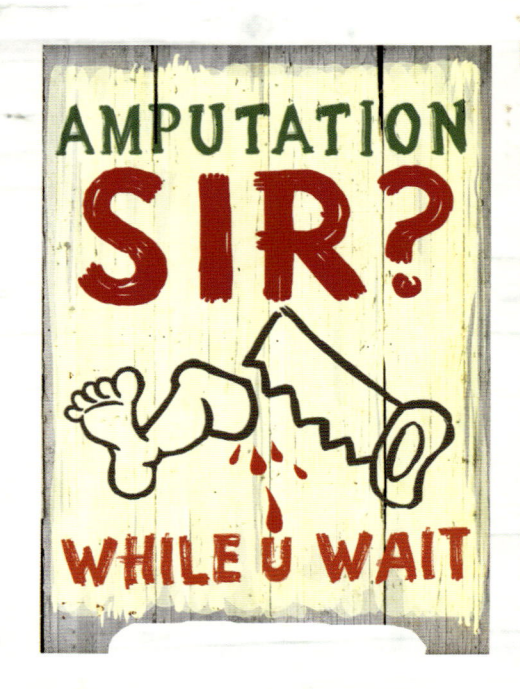

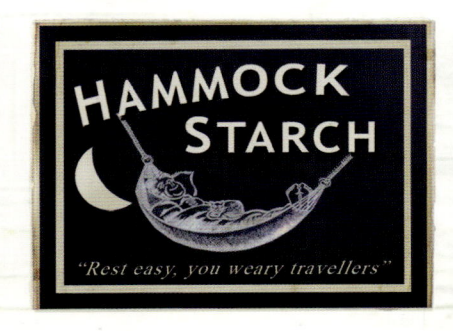

R. SPANKER MAST RAISERS & SHIP SUPPLIES
FUTTOCKS · ROLLOCKS · RIGGING · TACKLE

WORLD of HAM
SMOKED · HONEY ROASTED · BOILED · CHARGRILLED · OFF THE BONE · TEMPURA

AMPUTATION SIR?
WHILE U WAIT

Live SPORTS
Crab Racing this Thursday

EXCITING NEW MENU
LARGE GROG GARDEN

HAMMOCK Starch
"Rest easy, you weary travellers"

QUEEN VICTORIA WELCOMES YOU TO LONDON

100

Signs of the Times

KNOTS FOR THE FAINT-HEARTED and MONEY FOR KOLD ROPE are just two of the signs on Blood Island created by Supervising Graphic Designer Gavin Lines. 'Injecting the humour, that is the key thing,' says Gavin, talking about his contribution, which often takes the form of jokes and puns in the background or on the periphery of scenes.

Gavin was responsible not just for the signage in *The Pirates!* but for books, newspapers and magazines as well as wallpaper, carpets and the paintings and portraits on the walls of the Pirate Captain's cabin, the Queen's palace and the Royal Society. All of these pictures were printed on to canvas, treated with glaze and cracked in order to look antique.

This page and facing: signs designed by Gavin Lines and made by members of the props department

Mapping a Course

THE ELABORATELY DECORATED sea charts created by Supervising Graphic Designer Gavin Lines were inked by hand, scanned into a computer and then printed out on rough paper to give the authentic look of ancient parchment maps.

The Pirate Captain: Aah, confound it! We could have made that with a good wind behind us, but unfortunately there's this dirty great sea monster in the way.

Darwin: Um, I think they just add those on to maps for decoration, Captain.

Maps also provide a linking device in the film, with animated sequences of the ship sailing across charts and interacting with their features. In one scene, the 3D puppet Albino Pirate throws coloured floaters from the back of the ship that then become a dotted-line trail on the 2D animated map.

THIS PAGE AND FACING:
Centre:
Pirate map — Gavin Lines
Below left:
Title sequence map — Michael Schlingmann
All map decorations — Jonny Duddle

Victoriana

'**HISTORICAL REFERENCE IS** vitally important,' says Supervising Graphic Designer Gavin Lines, 'and it was an essential ingredient of the design process. In the *Wallace and Gromit* films, Aardman took the 1950s as an inspiration. For *The Pirates!* – despite the fact that it's a film that every now and again calls for a modern twist – we needed to base our designs solidly in the Victorian era.'

Gavin scoured libraries, ploughed through books and periodicals and surfed the internet in search of inspiration for London life in the 1800s that would add a richness of detail and texture to the sets. The results can be seen in every square, street and alleyway.

Far left: the Elephant Man (real-life Victorian, Joseph Merrick)
Right: London policemen or 'Peelers', named after the founder of the police force, Sir Robert Peel

CLOCKWISE FROM LEFT:
Artist | All illustrations by Jonny Duddle

Above left: studies for novelist Jane Austen
Drawings – Jonny Duddle
Armour – Diego Soriano Gomez

105

LIVE SPORTS
URCHIN THROWING
COCKNEY BAITING
FREEHOUSE
WALL (A)
350
100
350
100
350
100

VIII
Avast!
The Magic of Aardman

The animation of *The Pirates!*

A Painstaking Process

The art of animating

> Creating a believable performance is acting in slow motion!
> — *Ian Whitlock*, Animator

'THE CAPTAIN WAS dunking a custard cream in a cup of tea,' says Will Becher, recalling the first sequence he animated on *The Pirates!* 'I did a lot of testing for that shot – I must have got through at least eleven cups of tea and several packets of biscuits!'

The practicalities involved in creating that shot concern the basic process involved in stop-frame animation, as Animation Director Jay Grace explains: 'The animator starts by posing the puppet in its first position and takes a still single-image frame which is stored on a computer. The puppet is then moved into the next pose of the action and the animator takes another frame. That's it! Of course, the skill is knowing when to move things and when to leave things still and how to vary the speed of the puppet's actions to make the performance interesting and believable. That is where experience and practice are required.'

A vital part of preparation involves the animators acting out the scenes on video. 'This is a quick and effective way of exploring ideas,' says Jay. 'It's really spontaneous and we often discover fun and quirky mannerisms that we wouldn't necessarily have thought of that can be worked into the performance.'

For Suzy Parr, Queen Victoria's Lead Animator, preparation began with the script and the vocal recording: 'I played the voice track again and again until I was very familiar with it. There are so many ways a line can be performed that it is vital to understand how the actor interpreted it. When the Queen first meets the Pirate Captain, my priority was to establish her as a feared and dignified leader, but also as someone full of pent-up energy.'

Persuasively showing what might be going on in the head of a puppet is the true art of animation. 'When you get it right,' says Peter Lord, 'and you land a moment, or, better still, a whole series of moments, the audience is completely convinced that the puppet isn't just moving and talking, but is actually thinking! That's a great illusion and it's incredibly satisfying.'

Ian Whitlock, who had responsibility for Darwin and Mister Bobo, agrees: 'The eyes and eyebrows are where you see what a character is thinking – 80% of performance comes from that area.'

'I put tiny movements into the eyes,' says Will Becher, 'as if the puppet is unconsciously thinking; or I might slightly de-focus the eyes to replicate the glazed look of somebody in a daydream. Such detail helps create the illusion that the puppet is alive and performing for real, and gives Aardman characters their charm.'

Animating the mouth movements was made easier on *The Pirates!* by the use of the Rapid Prototype mouth replacements. 'It removed some of the pain of sculpting,' says Jay Grace, 'enabled us to shoot quicker and meant the characters stayed true to their model from one animator to another.'

Every sequence presents its own unique challenge: there might be other elements in a scene that will need to be animated, from background characters to objects such as swinging lanterns or a flag blowing in the wind.

However, as animator Lee Wilton explains, it is often the scenes that appear easiest that are the hardest to do: 'You might have a four-second shot of a character thinking, or giving a little look off-screen – it seems easy, but you have to make certain that the audience is interpreting it the way you're intending. Making it look effortless is very difficult.'

And that is the true mystery of the animator's art: 'You take a lump of clay,' says Animation Supervisor Loyd Price, 'and you breathe life into it. People respond to it as if it's a sentient being. That's what keeps you doing it. That's the buzz you get from doing it.'

Facing page: Will Becher, animating
Above: Frank Passingham (Director of Photography) and Jay Grace (animator) lining up a shot

110

The Art of Animating Emotion

'**Some animators might** be great at action sequences, others are great at believable character performances.' Animation Supervisor Loyd Price is describing the range of skills required to give life to the puppets in *The Pirates!*

The film's excitement may come from the fights, chases and action set pieces, but the characters' personalities are often created in scenes where nothing happens other than a conversation. Peter Lord points to the scene where the Pirate with a Scarf has to nudge the Pirate Captain out of his despair at being a failure: 'It took Will Becher over six months to animate and yet it plays out in just three minutes on screen, but the way the emotion builds organically is fantastic.'

Will Becher talks about filming this particular scene . . .

'Each shot in animation is created individually. Every time you move the camera, a huge amount of work goes into dressing the set and lighting the puppets. As a result – and unlike in live-action filming – we often shoot a conversation between two characters in two parts. On one stage, I have the Captain sitting in his cabin, downtrodden and feeling low; on another stage, twenty metres away, is the other half of the cabin and the Pirate with a Scarf trying to cheer him up.

'Peter Lord talks me through a storyboard version of the scene, explaining what's going through the characters' minds and how the audience is meant to be feeling. Then we act out the scene on video, taking it in turns to play the parts, in order to test the actions and timings for the shot, give Peter a chance to see what I have in mind and him the opportunity to show me what he wants in the scene. After discussions and notes, I shoot what we call a rough block-through of the action. Then more discussions, more notes and, possibly, tweaks to the lights and sets before the animation begins. The first frames sometimes feel like the hardest. I always need a cup of tea at this stage! Once the characters are moving and talking, it's a case of keeping the focus and working through to the end of the shot. It might be a 24-frame shot (one second of the film) or a 700-frame shot (almost half a minute). What is vitally important is that you understand what is required of the shot before you start animating because the worst-case scenario is that, after days or weeks, you finish the shot and the director isn't happy with it. In stop-motion a "Take Two" means going back to the very beginning and doing the whole shot again.'

AVAST! THE MAGIC OF AARDMAN

The Best Thing About Being a Pirate

THE AARDMAN CREW have had time to consider what some of the best things have been about having adventures with Pirates and Scientists. Here are a few of their thoughts in their own words . . .

It didn't matter that *The Pirates!* was a massive leap in terms of scale and complexity, the crew could always see what needed doing and we all just got on with our jobs.
— **Richard Beek**, Production Manager

My favourite bit was watching the script come to life with actors. Sitting in a theatre in Bristol, hearing it read out by clever, talented people. It gets you hugely excited. That's at the very start and it's really inspiring!
— **Julie Lockhart**, Producer

I'm really proud of the animation and the level of performance the team has achieved. Despite being close to the project I still marvel at the level of detail and I find that I'm totally immersed in the performance and forget that I'm watching a puppet, which is a fantastic thing.
— **Jay Grace**, Animation Director

It was magic to see the puppets we made being brought to life. Ian Whitlock animating Darwin with wonderful quirky expressions — it's an incredible feeling, as if the animator has got inside the character.
—*Andrew Bloxham*, Puppet Designer

I really enjoyed seeing Darwin come to life throughout the film. He's not always a likeable character, but hopefully he will stay in people's memories.
— **Ian Whitlock**, Animator

It's been a really enjoyable job and I am just fortunate to get to do it.
—*Gavin Lines*, Supervising Graphic Designer

> Nothing on screen is quite straight and true, so it needs to be created that way — if we needed a candlestick, we would sculpt it as opposed to using machinery to make it: the effect is subtle and tactile. The look of *Wallace and Gromit* was soft-edged; *The Pirates!* is hard-edged — everything has an edge to it but, though you may not notice it, none of those edges are straight.
> *—Matt Perry*, Supervising Art Director

I liked Queen Victoria's dual personality — especially the fact that she loses all that grace and dignity when she doesn't get what she wants!
– **Suzy Parr**, Animator

Nothing in the pirates' world exists until we create it — if you see a character holding a glass, that glass has had to be blown. So many people's skills and expertise came together to make a believable world and then draw the viewer into it.
– **Loyd Price**, Animation Supervisor

The biggest challenge? Getting things working and keeping them working. Writing software, solving problems, providing everything that's needed just before it's required to a standard that will enable a hugely complicated project to be achieved without restricting the artistic vision.
– **Tom Barnes**, Head of Camera and Lighting

My favourite moment: sequence 50, around shot 22; the open sea with two digital boats coming towards the camera with waves splashing and spraying around.
– **Andrew Morley**, Visual Effects Supervisor

It is challenging and fun at the same time. When your ideas on paper develop into a final rendered image on the big screen, that is brilliant.
– **Alfred Llupia Perez**, Digital Art Director

There are some sequences that work well in storyboard, telling the story and conveying the emotion in a shorthand form, but then the animators flesh out those moments, adding an extra layer of nuances to create something that is unrecognisably better than the storyboard.
– **Justin Kirsh**, Editor

We always knew the animation would be brilliant; that was a given. But when you get such quality characters and sets to light, that is an inspiration in itself. This made the project a real pleasure to work on.
– **Frank Passingham**, Director of Photography

Even small, simple scenes involve such a tremendous amount of labour and care. It's a fool's errand, but I am hugely proud to be part of something so insanely ambitious!
– **Theodore Shapiro**, Composer

I have had the luckiest time anyone could ever wish for: I've been creating worlds all my life, and I have a huge passion to carry on doing it. *The Pirates!* suited me down to the ground: whimsical, fanciful; one of the greatest experiences ever. Best bit? Scarlet Morgan hanging up in his cage — I love the stupidity of the humour!
– **Norman Garwood**, Production Designer

While working on *The Pirates!* I ate an average amount of ham and, at the very end, drank rather a lot of rum!
– **Will Becher**, Animator

What was unexpected was the amount of mouth shapes that were required (almost 7,000 by the end of the film) and the level of intricacy involved in painting them: each and every little mouth shape is beautiful.
– **Jacky Priddle**, Rapid Prototyping Production Manager

Reunion in The Barnacle's Face

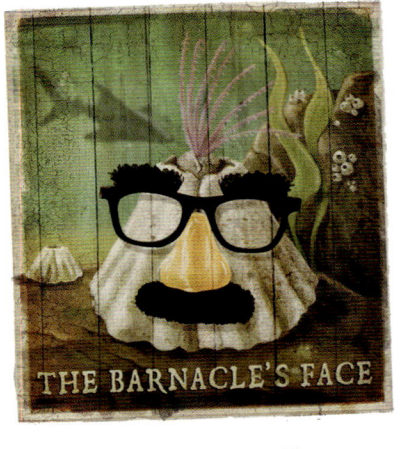

IT IS ONE of the longest scenes in the film and took eighteen months to shoot. The Pirate Captain and his crew are in The Barnacle's Face tavern on Blood Island where they are reintroduced to the other contenders for Pirate of the Year: Peg Leg Hastings, Cutlass Liz and Black Bellamy. With as many as sixteen pirates in the frame at any one moment, Character Lead Animator Christopher Sadler developed a method for dealing with that level of complexity: 'It's very easy to lose track of what you're doing when you're animating so many characters, so it helps to give them each their own story. For example: there's a table by the window in the tavern, where two are on a date, but a third is drunk and ruining it for them; there's a table where they're playing cards and one of them is cheating; and another where one of the pirates is drinking a cocktail and the other pirates are teasing him because they don't think it is piratey enough! It helps me to remember what to do, not to mention that it's nice to get a laugh going on in the background, away from the main action – that's a very Aardman thing.'

The arrival of the Pirate of the Year Award entrants at The Barnacle's Face tavern builds towards the ultimate entrance of the Pirate Captain's long-time nemesis: the most successful pirate on the Seven Seas and multiple winner of the award – Black Bellamy. A shameless show-off, Bellamy crashes the party in a huge sperm whale that smashes into the side of the tavern. In an outrageous pastiche of showbiz events, the whale's tongue unrolls like a red carpet. Bellamy fires a pistol into the whale, which 'churns out a huge stream of treasure, like a slot machine' and Bellamy surfs in on a sea of gold.

Facing page: animator Andy Symanowski
This page, above left: Peter Lord and Jeff Newitt discussing the texture of the whale's tongue.
Above right: a mock-up of the whale's mouth
Left: Paul Smith and Clive Scott lighting the tavern interior. Note the whale's tongue ready to unroll.

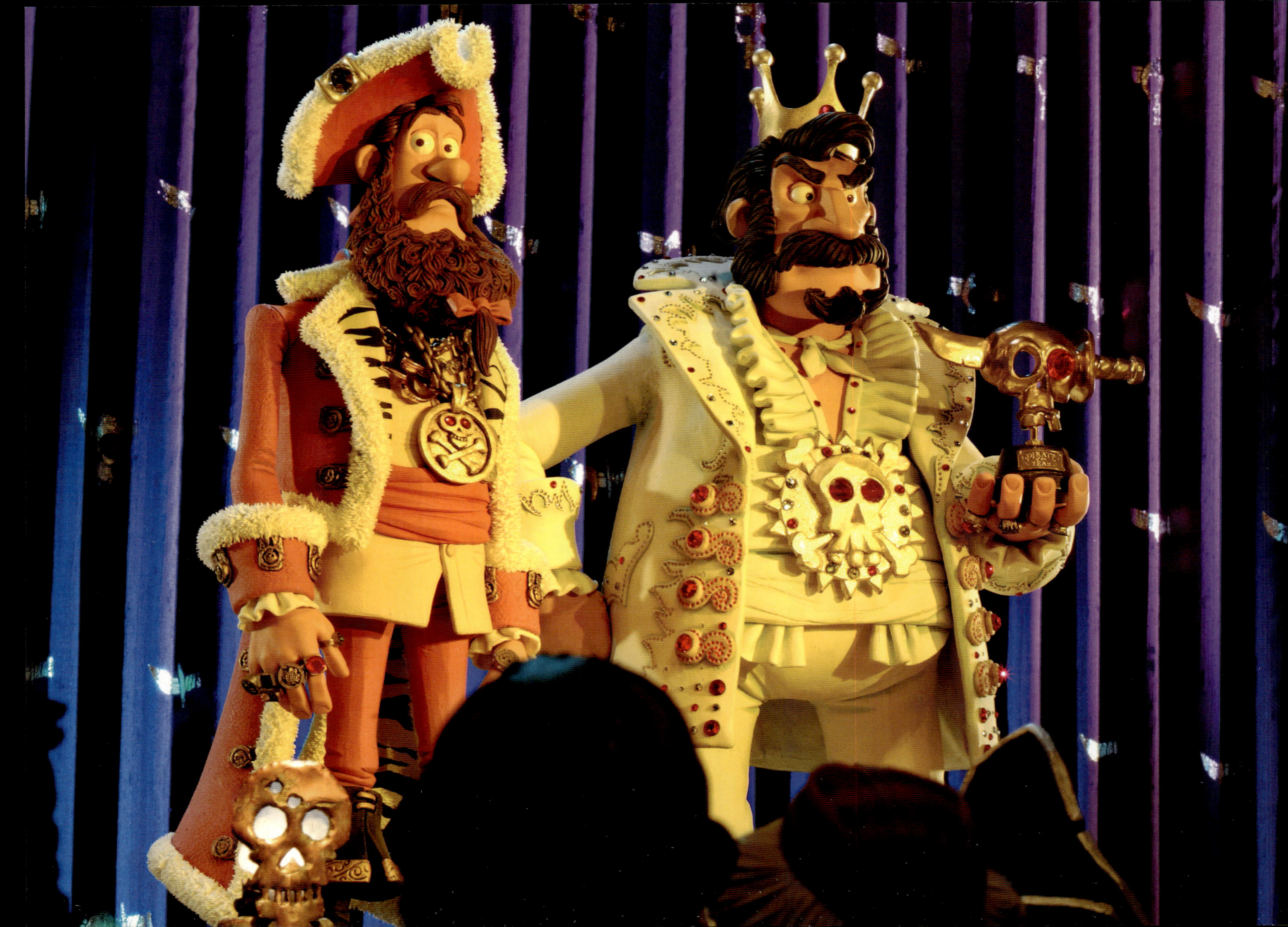

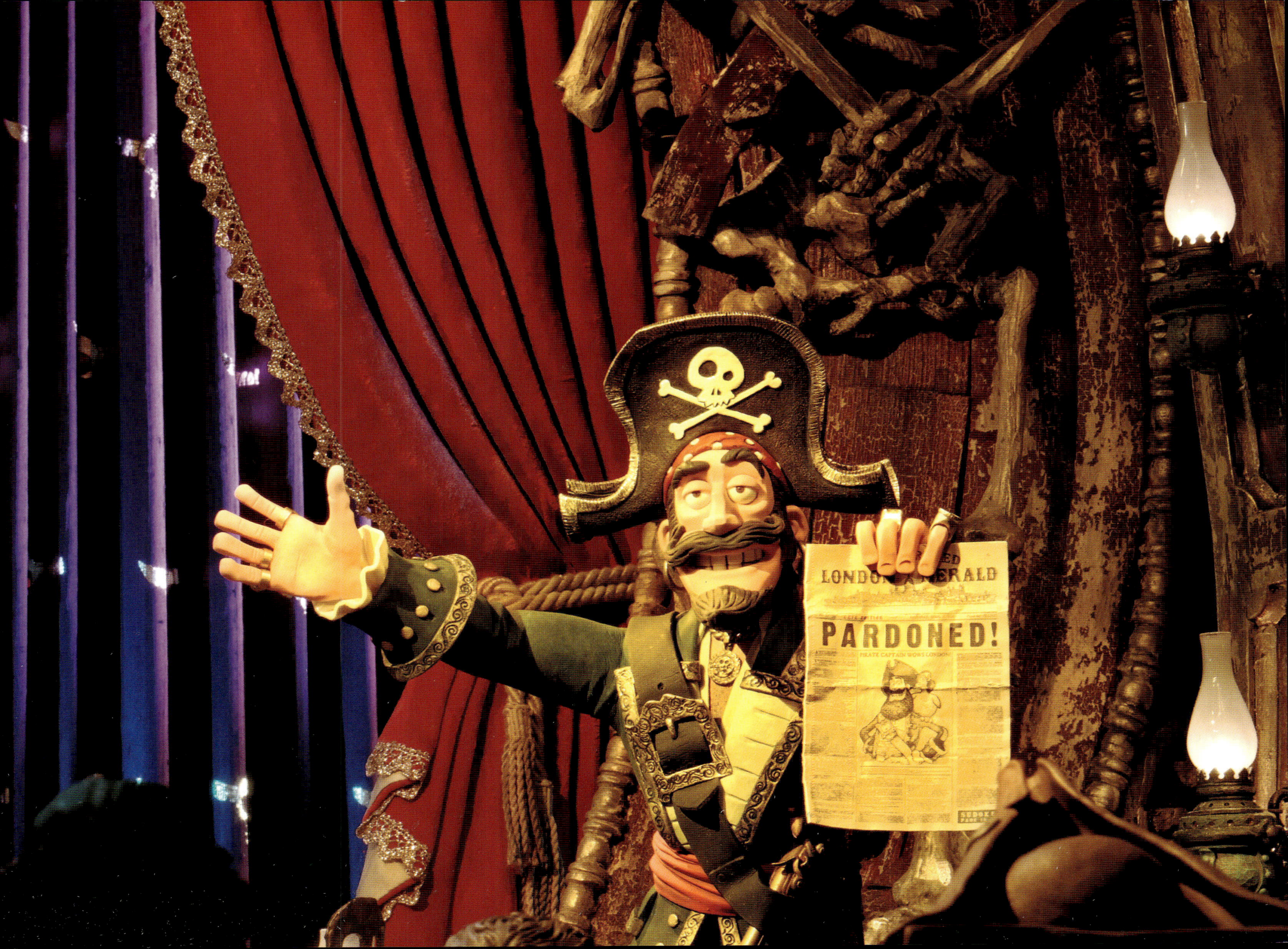
LONDON
PARDONED!

The Pirate of the Year Award

Any lubbers in tonight?

Above: Andrew Bloxham assembles the Captain after his 'makeover'.
Above right: Peter Lord and Phil Lewis in the theatre set

'**TO WIN IT** is almost a spiritual achievement,' says Brian Blessed, the voice of the Pirate King, talking about the Pirate of the Year Award. The character in his Elvis-style, rhinestone-embellished suit was animated by Laurie Sitzia-Hammond: 'I was really inspired by Brian's voice; I can't think of anyone more piratey!'

Discussing the Pirate Captain's obsession with the Award, his voice talent, Hugh Grant, observes: 'He has entered many times but has always come in last. You win by having the most booty, but his booty haul is always tragic!'

Himself a multi-award-winner, Hugh Grant says of the Pirate of the Year Award: 'It's like a sort of Oscar® for pirates,' and the glitzy, Las Vegas-style ceremony on Blood Island (hosted by the Pirate King) provided the film-makers with an opportunity to create a memorable set piece of imaginative design and comic animation.

Laurie also created the dance sequence that opened the Awards show. 'It involved a lot of leg kicking, sidestepping, jazzy hands, and big cheesy grins. I spent a few days testing with one of the peg-legged pirates to see what worked best, then, once I'd choreographed the routine, I shot all three of them on the theatre set. I had to access the puppets on stage through a hole in the floor and, being surrounded by 360 degrees of the beautiful miniature theatre, I felt like Alice in Wonderland.'

Left: Ludovi Berardo animating in the theatre set. At the top of the shot, delicately positioned lights, mirrors and 'flags' help to imitate the effect of candlelight and lamplight in the darkened theatre.
Above: the Pirate King offers the Pirate of the Year award. An elaborate rig – which will be out of shot – helps to move the award in tiny increments.

Jay Grace (**above**) and Laurie Sitzia-Hammond (**below**), animating

Speaking Likenesses

'**THE PIRATE CAPTAIN**,' says Hugh Grant, who provides his voice, 'is a big, portly, bearded, luxuriant fellow and that just isn't me. Of course, I didn't have to play him physically – it was my voice they wanted.'

Describing the process of casting actors in the vocal roles, Julie Lockhart says: 'Regardless of a performer's dramatic or comedic qualities, the voice itself needs to be convincing and have a quality that will suit the character. You have to separate the voice from all other associations, listen to it almost as if it were a disembodied voice and try to picture it coming out of your character's mouth. That, coupled with a great performance and comic timing, makes the perfect voice.'

It is a view shared by Imelda Staunton, who voices Queen Victoria: 'You can't pull faces, your voice is all you've got. To rely on your voice is a good place to be as an actor, because that's where it all is – your heart and soul has to be heard, rather than looked at.'

The collaborative relationship between voice and animator is hugely important to the success of the character on screen, as the Lead Animator for

> We avoided typical pirate voices because we thought of this as a comedy with pirates, not a pirate movie that happened to be funny.
> – *Julie Lockhart*, Producer

'This Queen Victoria has more than a couple of screws missing,' says Imelda Staunton, who provided voices for previous Aardman films *Chicken Run* and *Arthur Christmas*, and returned to give voice to the pirate-hating monarch.

Right: Queen Victoria with her voice, Imelda Staunton and animator Suzy Parr

Queen Victoria, Suzy Parr, explains: 'Observing how Imelda moved and talked – noting her upright posture and clear diction – played a huge part in the way her character was developed.'

Darwin's Lead Animator, Ian Whitlock, had a similar experience: 'The biggest breakthrough for me was seeing the footage of David Tennant recording his lines. His performance touched so many areas – quirky and stumbly, confident, nervous, sinister and smarmy – and he moved in a weird, unexpected way that unlocked how to play him.'

All the actors need to make an emotional investment in their modelling clay alter egos, as Brian Blessed, voice of the Pirate King, explains: 'You cannot allow yourself to think of the characters as puppets. They must be totally real. I visited the Aardman studios and was able to place the Pirate King on the set with my own hands. That was magical and I used the moment of holding the figure to infuse myself into it.'

And for Hugh Grant, the Pirate Captain puppet provided a solution for how to interpret the role vocally: 'Aardman had already modelled the character when they approached me about the part, so it was quite a challenge: I had to model myself to him rather than the other way around. The way in was through his eyes; whatever else an Aardman character has, they all have a kind of wide-eyed innocence. The strange thing is that I have several young cousins who have seen the film and love it but insist that it's not my voice!'

Right: 'I got to the studios half an hour early,' says Brian Blessed. 'I warmed myself up so my adrenaline was very, very high. I could only get the Pirate King right if I was superlative.'

Above: David Tennant recording the voice for Charles Darwin, and the puppet character demonstrating a remarkably Tennant-like gesture.

Blink and You'll Miss It

A Treasure Trove of Trivia

IT HAS ALWAYS been the Aardman tradition to include lots of quirky and amusing little details that often get missed on the first viewing. More than any of their previous films, *The Pirates!* is jam-packed full of gags – some quite hard to spot. Here are a few things to keep your eyes open for the next time you watch the film – including one or two where the joke is that they shouldn't really be there . . .

• In addition to the usual features found on the deck of a pirate ship there is that handy bad-weather accessory, an umbrella stand, and the door to the Captain's cabin has a cat flap-style 'Polly flap'!

• There is a salad bar in The Barnacle's Face tavern on Blood Island.

• In the Hook Line and Sinker inn, there are beer mugs with the faces of Director Peter Lord and Co-Director Jeff Newitt.

• In the after-show party at the Royal Society, there is a painting on the wall of the Clifton Suspension Bridge in Bristol, a local landmark in Aardman's home city.

• Look closely during the scene in Queen Victoria's treasure room and you may spot a gold Shaun the Sheep and Wallace and Gromit.

AVAST! THE MAGIC OF AARDMAN

- Odd household items collected by the pirates that hold the ship together include a broom and a cricket bat.

- There are yellow sticky notes stuck up in the Pirate Captain's cabin.

- Director Peter Lord has a brief cameo in the film as the policeman who lifts his hat (revealing a sandwich underneath) and says, 'Mind how you go, ladies.'

- In the galley of the Pirates' ship, you can see the pirates' chutney and jam collection. Another shelf is labelled 'Medicines and Poisons'.

- There is a bumper sticker on the back of the ship that says: 'Honk if you're seasick.'

- In Queen Victoria's lair, the suits of armour have the shapes of a corgi dog, Scarf, Gout and the Surprisingly Curvaceous Pirate.

- The Tower of London, where the Pirate Captain goes looking for Polly, did once house a royal menagerie, although the last of the animals had been moved to London Zoo in Regent's Park in 1835, two years before Victoria came to the throne.

- Although the imposing dining room where we first encounter Queen Victoria is supposed to be in Buckingham Palace, the view from the window suggests that it is actually located south of the River Thames.

- When passing Scarlet Morgan hung up in a cage on Execution Dock, the Pirate Captain makes the 'Call Me' gesture.

- In the bedroom in Darwin's house, the Pirate with a Scarf switches off the lights, but since the room was lit by candles and gaslight that couldn't possibly have happened.

- The film is supposedly set in 1836 but we see London's Tower Bridge, which wasn't completed until 1895.

- The Pirate with Gout wears a *Blue Peter* badge on his hat. The badge, with its ship insignia, is awarded by the world's longest-running children's television programme, *Blue Peter*. In maritime signalling, the Blue Peter flag signifies that all are aboard and the vessel is about to proceed to sea. The badge was designed by TV presenter and artist Tony Hart and it was on his programme, *Take Hart*, that Aardman's modelling-clay character, Morph, made his debut in 1977. Aardman's Nick Park is one of the distinguished group to have been awarded a gold Blue Peter badge.

- In the royal kitchen on the *QV1*, there is an elephant's foot kebab roasting on the spit.

- Unlike most ships, the one owned by the Pirates has no name!

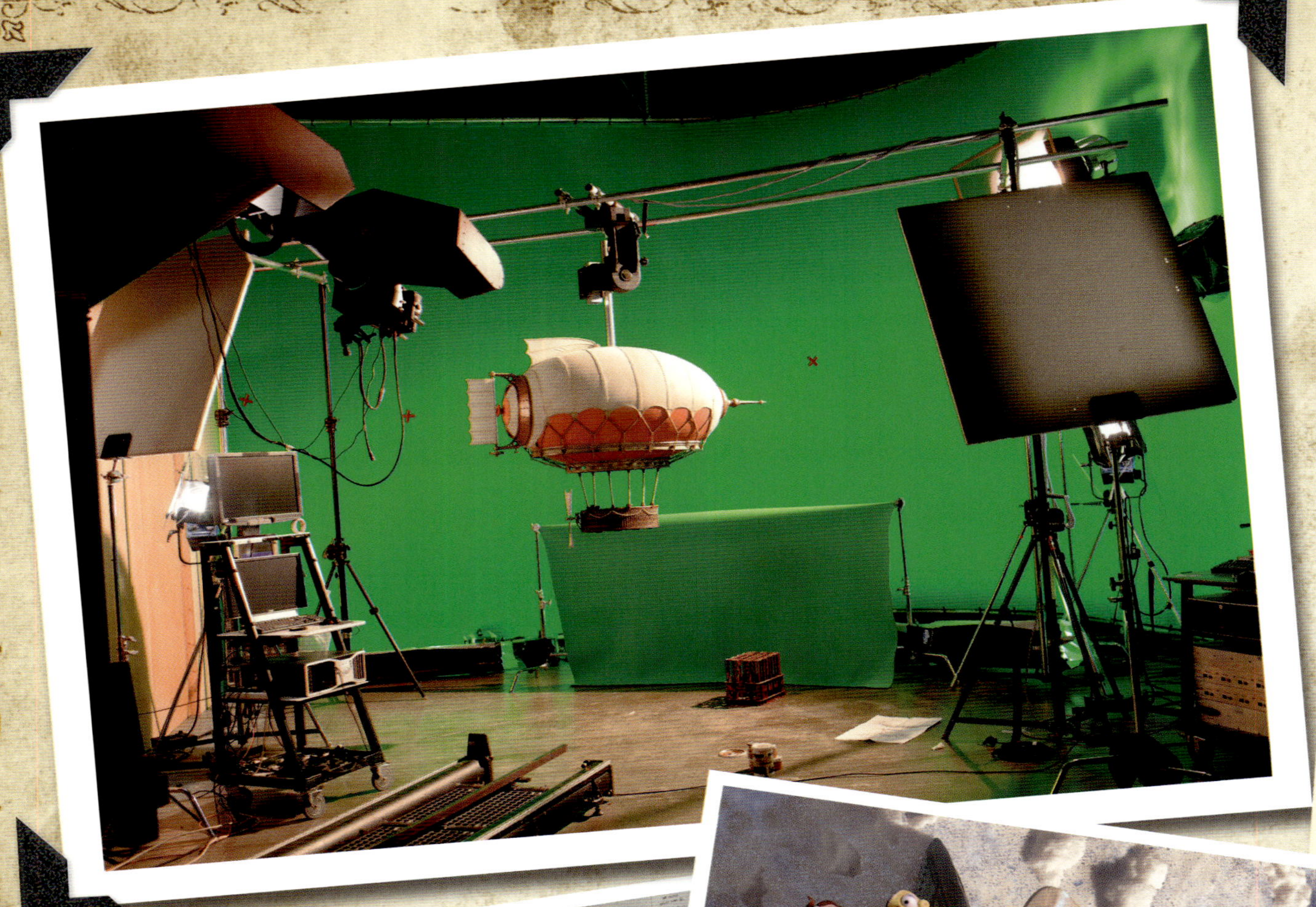

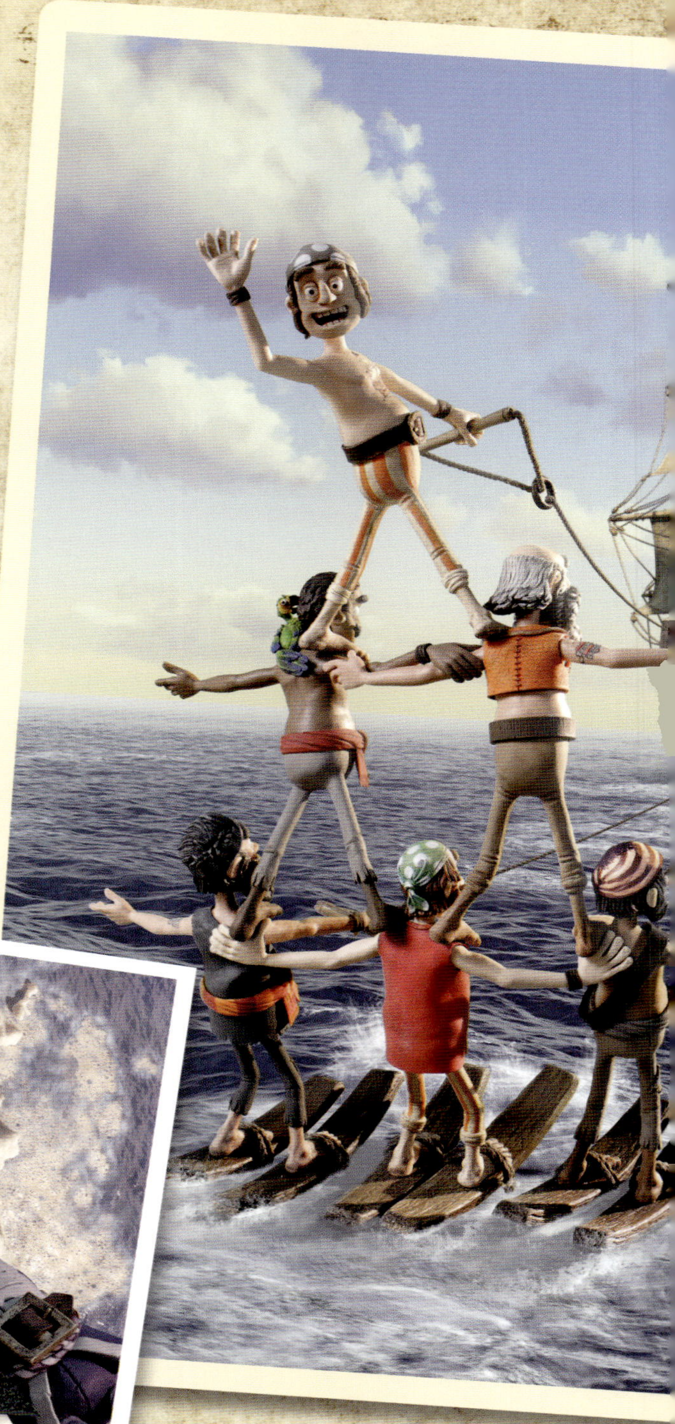

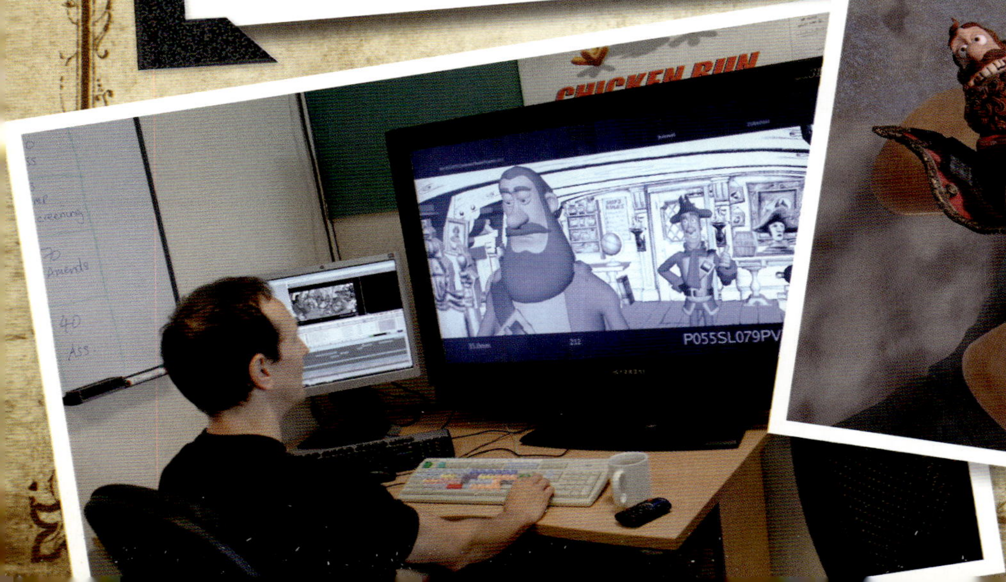
P055SL079PV

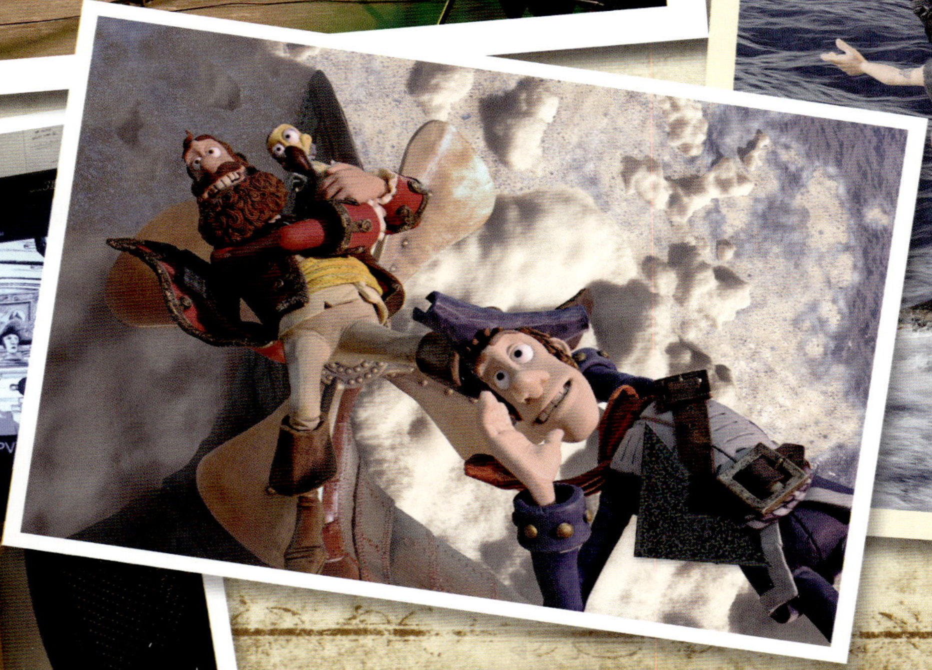

IX
Baking Soda and a Beautiful Briny Sea

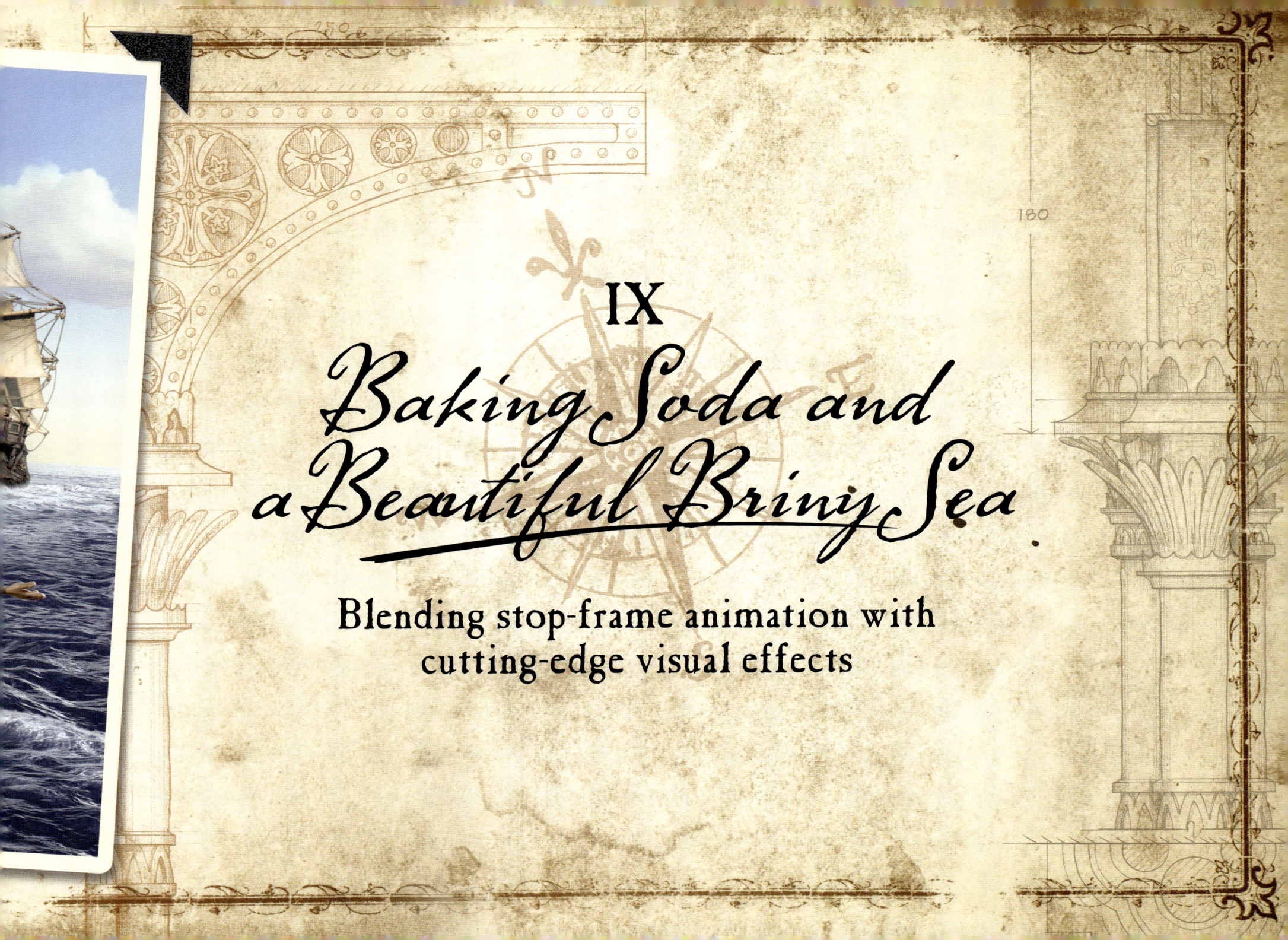

Blending stop-frame animation with cutting-edge visual effects

BAKING SODA AND A BEAUTIFUL BRINY SEA

Visually Effective

An Adventure with Special Effects

> I describe it as digital modelling clay. Everything you see needs to be built; *our tools are simply the mouse, keyboard and monitor.*
>
> —*Andrew Morley*, Visual Effects Supervisor

'IN MANY WAYS,' says Director Peter Lord, 'we are animating in the same way as has been done for fifty years, but in *The Pirates!* we combined those techniques with state-of-the-art visual effects and computer animation.' Although earlier Aardman films have included some visual effects, they were always previously provided by a London-based company. For *The Pirates!* the decision was taken to establish a dedicated in-house effects facility.

During pre-production, computer animation played an essential role by creating a pre-visualisation (pre-vis) version of the film in which the storyboard drawings were converted into something that Editor Justin Kirsh refers to as looking like 'wonky black-and-white Computer Graphic animation'. Playing in real time, pre-vis is intended as a tool to aid the directors in planning sets and shots. As Justin explains: 'CG animation works by constructing images from polygons: the more you have, the smoother it looks – but the longer it takes. If we need to work quickly, which we do when creating a pre-vis, we use far fewer polygons, so the result is very basic. The characters don't show any emotions, the animation simply walks them through the space. Nevertheless, it's still a lengthy process and with 64,246 storyboard sketches to be turned into three-dimensional images, it sometimes felt like we were never going to get to the end of them!'

Pre-vis not only helped Peter Lord and Co-Director Jeff Newitt identify which shots in the film required additional visual effects, but also enabled them to distinguish between those that were to be traditionally animated and those created using computer graphics.

CG Supervisor Ted Chaplin says: 'Anything that was too big to build – from sea monsters and whales to the larger ships – had to be created by our department and made to look as if it had been crafted on the set and was actually there.'

BAKING SODA AND A BEAUTIFUL BRINY SEA

Visual Effects Supervisor Andrew Morley explains the process: 'Although we used computers, we went through the same linear process as the stop-frame animators. We started with a camera layout to mimic what had been shot on the set, followed by a "world, layout", where we put all the elements in the shot before animating and painting. In the digital world, you often make the images in lots of layers, a process called rendering; after that comes the compositing, when the images are joined up, the layers stitched together and any problems fixed.'

In addition to sequences requiring elaborate assistance from the computer graphic artists, every single shot in the film featuring puppets had to pass through the Visual Effects department. Because the characters had mouth components fitted to their faces there were tell-tale lines revealing where they were attached – all of which had to be digitally removed.

Despite the reliance on new technology, there was, says Peter Lord, an overriding philosophy: 'We were determined that we would never get away from those qualities that audiences love about stop-frame animation.'

Agreeing, Ted Chaplin says: 'This film was on a much bigger scale than anything Aardman had ever done before, and our job was to give the visual effects as much love and attention as goes into the sets and characters that are built on the shop floor. That was the most important thing – to make the CG match the Aardman world. We didn't want the audience to lose that suspension of disbelief when they're watching the film, no matter how it's animated.'

Facing page: Paul Faulkner and Rebecca Rose creating the pre-vis
Above: Mike Shirra in the Visual Effects department

When Worlds Combine

Merging Stop-frame and CGI

'**I AM FIERCELY** defensive of what we do,' says Peter Lord of the studio's famed stop-frame animation techniques, 'it is a big part of the appeal and pleasure of watching our films. But, in our medium, some things – such as crowds of extras and massive landscapes – are either incredibly difficult and costly or just downright impossible.'

The solution was to combine traditional stop-frame animation with effects made possible by cutting-edge computer technology. For example, confronted by the challenge of creating Blood Island, the film-makers built the harbour and left the computer graphic artists to create the exotic location using a process called Chroma Key Compositing. More simply known as 'green screen', this involved filming the model buildings along the quayside in front of green screens. The camera is programmed to view green areas as being transparent, allowing the computer graphic team to subsequently add in the appropriate background. 'For a director,' says Peter, 'it is great! I can point the camera anywhere I like, knowing that everything else will added later.'

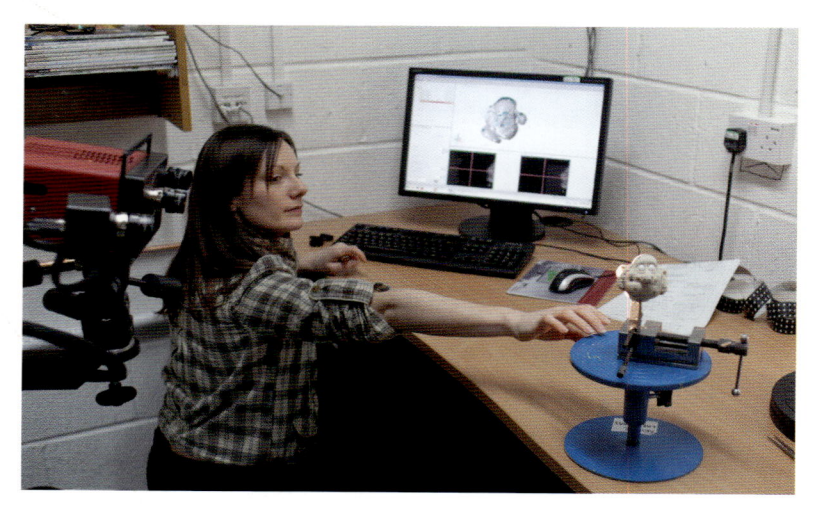

Digital Art Director Alfred Llupia Perez explains how he worked with the director: 'Once the concept art for the Island's appearance had been approved, Peter would decide on the camera angles he wanted for the shots and I made quick sketches. Then I started work producing a digital background first in black and white to give depth and light, before adding the necessary colour and textures to create the final image to be seen on screen.'

On the return to Blood Island for the Pirate of the Year Awards, the skills of stop-frame and digital animators were again united, this time to fill the theatre with an audience of enthusiastic buccaneers. A group of twenty cheering pirate puppets were animated by Ludovic Berardo for the foreground – in itself no mean achievement – who were later joined by a horde of digital extras. Peter Lord describes the result: 'The scene came back populated by another hundred whistling, stamping pirates – the almost deserted theatre became a rowdy, noisy place crammed with life. I have never seen

Left: Helen Duckworth, working in the Visual Effects department
Right: character mouths were animated in CG and later printed out with Rapid Prototyping.
Far right: puppets in front of a green screen are joined by hordes of CG pirates to complete the scene (below).

anything like that in puppet animation before.'

A similar effect – with a rather more sober audience of Scientists – featured in the scenes set in the Royal Society. On the studio floor, the set built for the auditorium featured a dozen puppets in front of ranks of empty seats that were subsequently filled by dozens of digital Victorians. 'I can't imagine,' says Peter, 'a world where we could ever have had the time or money to make enough puppets for such a scene – let alone be able to reach them all and animate them.'

For many of the other London sequences, elaborate sets were constructed with cobbled streets, gas lamps and model buildings standing at around 1.8m high. That, however, was not enough for Director Peter Lord: 'We wanted the camera to be able to see over the tops and past the edges of the houses. Since, once more, we couldn't physically build all of that, we used CG imagery to make the world bigger by digitally adding rooftops and smoking chimney pots.'

Reflecting on the enhanced use of digital technologies, Peter says: 'Through the contribution of our VFX and CG teams, we've been able to free ourselves and step into a bigger environment of vast locations and masses of characters, and fully enjoy the visual potential. Seeing these two worlds come together has been thrilling – and, what's more, even I can't see the join!'

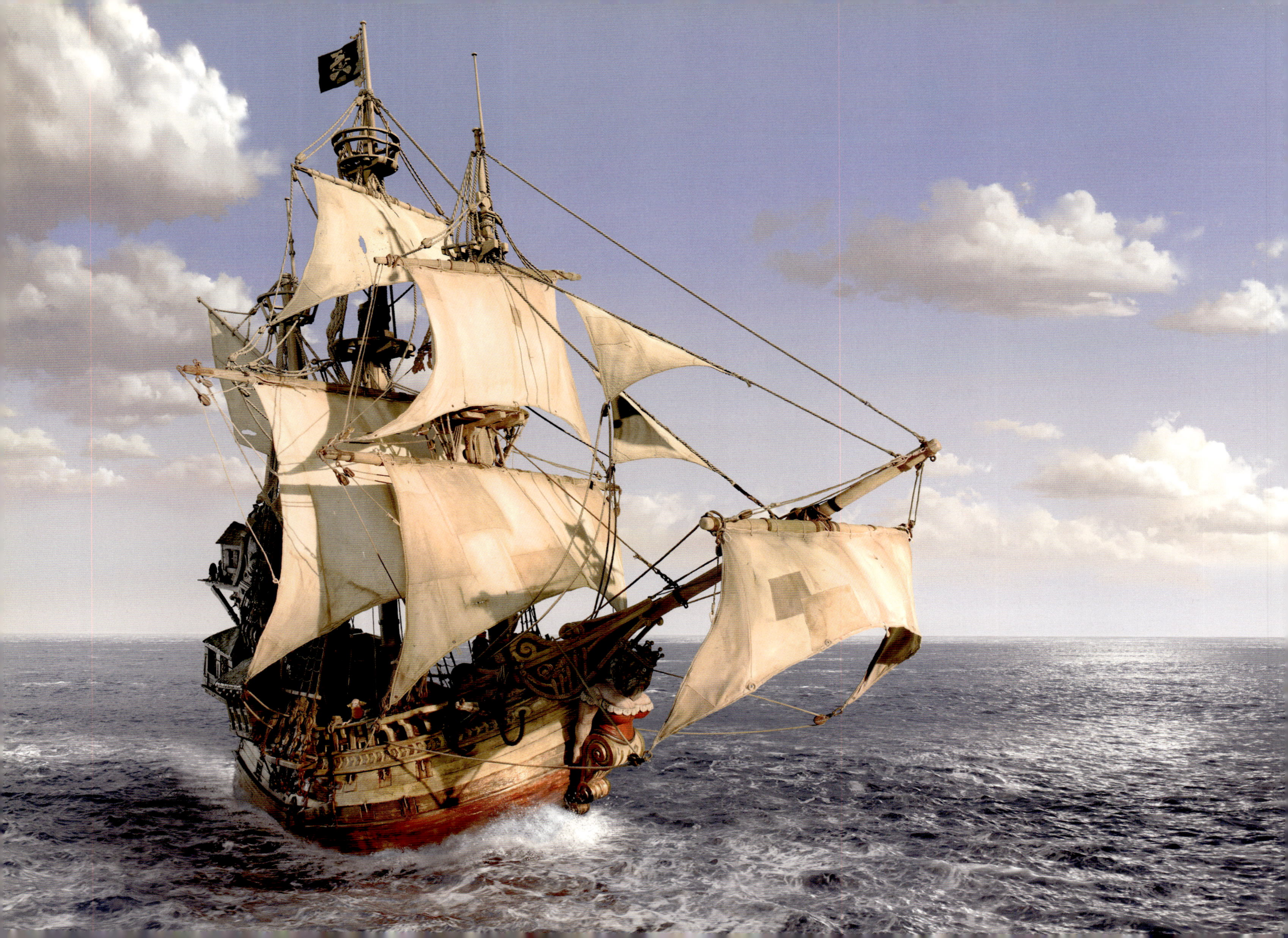

Splashtastic!

Creating the Aardman Ocean

There's nothing I like more than the classic pirate image of a great big ship thrashing into a wave, sinking, splashing, and rising above. – *Peter Lord,* Director

IF THERE WAS one thing that could easily have scuppered *The Pirates! In an Adventure with Scientists!* it was the inescapable need for the film to feature water – by the oceanful.

Creating a sea in stop-frame animation may have been an impossible task, but providing a computer graphics alternative was still a considerable challenge for the visual effects artists, not least because the relevant computer software is designed for live-action film-makers wanting photo-realistic perfection. The Aardman world is real in as much as physical puppets on model sets are manipulated by hand and photographed with a camera; but it is also a world with a look that is, intentionally, neither 'realistic' nor 'perfect' and is greatly admired for those qualities.

'We were going after something a bit more handmade,' says Visual Effects Supervisor Andrew Morley. 'It needed to look and move mostly like water, but also to have an Aardman charm. So we wrote an in-house water simulation tool for the wide-to-medium shots. For the closer shots, we were able to use existing software, but even then, we decided not to animate fine spray, as you'd see in waves crashing against rocks – the words we used were "chunkier spray".'

The stop-frame animators filmed the model ships using a computer-controlled mechanical rig to make it move as if it were on water and then passed the shots to the Visual Effects department. 'To start with,' says Andrew, 'we didn't touch the computer! We sat down with Supervising Art Director Matt Perry and Director of Photography Frank Passingham and looked through loads of images of the kind found in holiday brochures to give the director a menu of visual options.'

Wherever the digital sea had to interact with real objects such as a boat or a harbour wall, the real elements had to be digitally replicated along with the water in order for the two to coexist. In less complex shots, creating a sea comes down to a mathematical formula to give the classic wave look with various additional images – such as foam – projected on top. 'If you think of the crest of a wave,' Andrew explains, 'it often has a white tip to it. We could do stuff with that. We had more of what animators call "squash and stretch" than you get with real water – this enabled us to create a look that was a little bit modelling clay-like, as if it were something that could have been done by the model makers.'

A good deal of trial and error was involved: 'To start, there was a lot of back and forth. Once we had done two or three sequences, however, we began to get the feel for it. We had a test shot that we called "crashing through waves" involving masses of spray and foam, which looked so good that Peter Lord insisted we find a place for it in the final film.'

Polishing up the Diamond

Editing, Sound and Music

THE ANIMATION HAD been completed and the visual effects were all added, but there was still work to be done before *The Pirates!* could be launched on to the sea of movie releases.

A final edit had yet to be completed, although this process had, effectively, been under way since the earliest stages of production, as Editor Justin Kirsh explains: 'Editing animation is completely different from editing live action. In an animated film, the great part of editing is done before anything is shot, when we cut the film together for the first time using the storyboard sketches to make a story-reel. It goes through a second edit when we make the pre-vis and, as a result, there are rarely any spare frames to throw away at the end. By that point, editing is about putting sequences together so that they make sense – it is about telling the story.'

An important part of that storytelling is the use of sound, and the task of finding or creating those sounds is a vital and imaginatively demanding one, as Supervising Sound Editor Adrian Rhodes explains: 'Our job is to build a sound world that helps support and bring to life the characters by planting them in their various environments, but without getting in the way. One of the toughest scenes was the saucepan and sword fight between Queen Victoria and the Pirate Captain: squeezing in a wealth of shings, tings, bangs, crashes, splatters, swishes and whooshes to generate thrills and excitement whilst leaving space for the dialogue was challenging.'

The source of a sound is not always what it might seem to be to the ear: the sound of real sea tended to be too hissy and lacking necessary detail, so the oceans in the film are a combination of recordings made at a reservoir and various swimming pools.

'For the tumbling wine barrel sequence,' says Adrian, 'we purchased some genuine wine barrels which we recorded being dropped and rolling along, but it was not that impressive so we enhanced the sound by bashing other wooden and metal props. Many sound effects were recorded around our own homes where there's always a wealth of props available, and the results are then bent, twisted and shaped using various electronic gizmos. I discovered, for example, that rolling socked feet over a particularly old heavy coffee table produced wonderful ship-like creaks.'

Whilst the actors all returned for a final polish

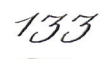

of their dialogue, recording line changes and adding grunts and groans, one voice had to be created completely from scratch. 'Polly was tricky,' Adrian recalls. 'We had to give her a nice character and some ability to convey emotion, but also make her sound like an extinct bird.'

The final Polly sounds were selected from a combination of vocal utterances from Adrian and colleagues, Sound Effects Editor Anthony Bayman and Dialogue Editor Tim Hands: 'We squawked like parrots, cooed like pigeons and honked like geese constricting our throats to emulate a bird-sized voice. Then we changed the pitch, reversed the recordings, added warble and sampled the results on a keyboard.'

Adrian's favourite sound? No contest: the censoring elephant trumpet that accompanies Mr Bobo's '@★#!' flashcard.

The final embellishment was when a 95-piece orchestra recorded the music score by Theodore Shapiro in London's famous Abbey Road Studios. However, as the composer explains, the process had begun long before: 'When I joined the project, they were in the midst of shooting. I began with one or two ideas, threw around a few thematic concepts, giving them time to live with the music, think about it and react to it before I began writing the score.'

Describing his finished compositions, Theodore says: 'There is a nice ragtag, piratey tonality to the score with guitars, clanging percussion and some unique sounds. When I first visited Aardman in Bristol, Peter Lord gave me important guidance about the tone; his big idea was that this was a bunch of kind-hearted, genuine, mischievous pirates, who were simply trying to be the best they could be. To me, that said a lot about the ethos of the film and the guiding principles that have imbued all the work we've done.'

Above left: the orchestra records the score for *The Pirates!* at the famous Abbey Road Studios.
Above right: composer Theodore Shapiro at the recording

FROM THE CREATORS OF 'CHICKEN RUN'
LAUGH YOUR BOOTY OFF
BLOOD ISLAND PIRATE SUPPLIES
TNT
UH-OH!
The PIRATES!
BAND OF MISFITS
IN 3D
COLUMBIA PICTURES AND SONY PICTURES ANIMATION PRESENT AN AARDMAN PRODUCTION 'THE PIRATES! BAND OF MISFITS' HUGH GRANT DAVID TENNANT IMELDA STAUNTON MARTIN FREEMAN JEREMY PIVEN
CO-DIRECTOR JEFF NEWITT MUSIC BY THEODORE SHAPIRO EXECUTIVE PRODUCER CARLA SHELLEY
BASED UPON THE BOOK 'THE PIRATES! IN AN ADVENTURE WITH SCIENTISTS' BY GIDEON DEFOE SCREENPLAY BY GIDEON DEFOE
PRODUCED BY PETER LORD DAVID SPROXTON JULIE LOCKHART
DIRECTED BY PETER LORD
Aardman
PG PARENTAL GUIDANCE SUGGESTED
SOME MATERIAL MAY NOT BE SUITABLE FOR CHILDREN
MILD ACTION, RUDE HUMOR AND SOME LANGUAGE
ThePirates-Movie.com
APRIL 27

X
This Can Only End Brilliantly

Pulling everything together

THIS CAN ONLY END BRILLIANTLY

Setting Sail

> To cut a long story short, *The Pirates!* was completed on time and on budget – amazing considering how huge a project it was. – *Richard Beek*, Production Manager

THE FILM MIGHT have been, as they say, 'in the can', but a great deal still remained to be done as the release date drew ever nearer. As Producer Julie Lockhart says, 'We had to let the outside world know what we were doing,' – and that meant getting publicity for the film was of paramount importance. Trailers were edited and shown in cinemas and on the internet; images from key moments in the film were selected and made available to newspapers and periodicals; logos, posters and advertisements were designed; merchandising deals were made and commercial tie-ins agreed. Preview screenings were arranged for journalists and critics in the media and, finally, a glamorously glitzy premiere gave the pirates a memorable send-off on their adventures.

Above: *The Pirates!* Director Peter Lord at the New York premiere with some of the film's characters
Right: the British poster for the film

THIS CAN ONLY END BRILLIANTLY

Looking back, Julie reflects on her involvement in the film: 'Nobody really knows what a producer does! The skill in my role is to find the best people for the jobs that have to be done, and it is exhilarating seeing the buzz of excitement as the crew comes together. As the project progressed, problem-solving became a big element of my job. I had to make sure all the cross-communications between departments were working and that things didn't stray too far from the path creatively. I was, alternately, keeping people's fears at bay and ensuring that the team spirit kept going. It is a very difficult line to tread, but it is essential to safeguard the creative content and make sure that any compromises don't make people feel compromised.'

Summing up, Julie says: 'Our aim was always that the film we had at the end was the film we set out to make. That we managed to do it, that we brought this in on time and on budget, never ceases to amaze me. But, quite simply, that is down to an amazing team, their passion for the project and their dedication and determination to produce such a fantastic film.'

Left: the Captain and the Director – Hugh Grant and Peter Lord, attending the film's premiere in New York.

Above and below: *The Pirates!* go plundering around the world.

Staggering Statistics

Ooooh! Maths!
– The Albino Pirate

- There were 525 people on the film crew, including 31 animators working in 41 shooting units in 4 studios.

- Animators averaged 3 seconds of animation completed per week.

- The film features 112 characters, represented by 340 puppets made by 70 model-makers.

- The Pirate Captain's beard has 65 swirls on it and 5 beard designs. He also has 7 costume changes and 257 different mouth shapes to convey his speech and reactions.

- Over 6,818 puppet mouths were created, including 1,364 for the Pirate Captain.

- The pirate ship could tilt and roll up to ten degrees from the horizontal, moving at 0.5 degrees per second.

- 140 sets of eyelids were created for the key pirate crew.

- 30,000 lentils were glued on to the hull of the *QV1* to simulate rivets.

- The pirate ship model is 425cm long from bowsprit to the tail end of the rudder and 450cm tall from the keel to the top of the tallest mast. Weighing 350kg, it is made of 44,569 individual parts – plus over 400m of rope.

- More than 220,000 props were created to fill the film's sets, including an array of miniature bottles, lamps and glasses custom-made by a specialist glass-blower.

- The avalanche of wealth in Queen Victoria's treasure room is made up of over 400,000 glittering gold coins.

- 50 packs of baby wipes were used to clean the puppets, and supplies of KY Jelly were used to simulate water effects.

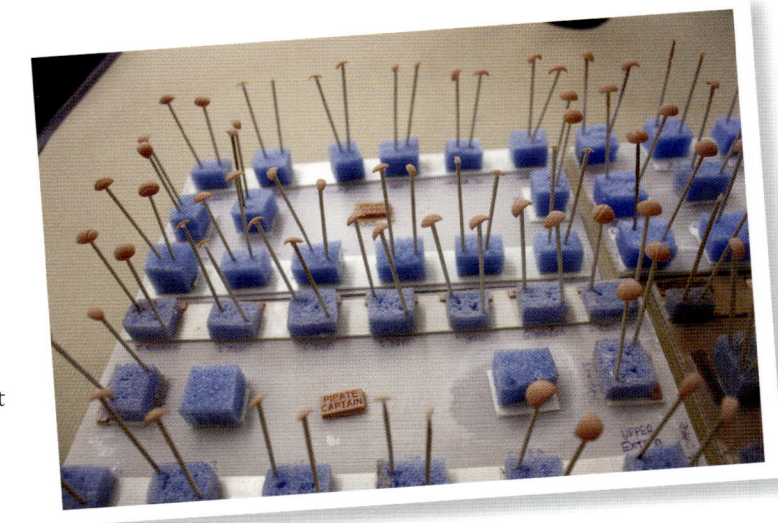

- Approximate catering statistics for the crew include:

Sandwiches made	28,000
Sausages eaten	6,900
Croissants consumed	20,000
Hot lunches cooked	56,000
Potatoes peeled	5,100kg
Chips fried	120,000
Squash (undiluted!) made up	10,700 l
Teabags brewed	120,200

Afterword by David Sproxton

AS I WRITE this piece *The Pirates! In an Adventure with Scientists!* is just coming to the end of its cinema run in Europe, thus concluding a journey that started almost five years ago. However, the real journey started almost forty years ago, when Peter Lord and I first met at school as young teenagers. Casting my mind back to the sketches and drawings which populated Peter's notebooks during his school career, pictures which featured strong, characterful figures like swashbucklers, cowboys, highwaymen and the like, I can only conclude that what the film *The Pirates!* represents is the culmination of a lifetime of sketching, observation, writing and study. The film is almost the manifestation of his soul!

Of course, the journey has been long and at times arduous, but the experience gained on that journey has certainly paid off. *The Pirates!* is a wonderful celebration of the medium of stop-frame animation and combined with the wonders of modern technology, puts before the audience a film the like of which has never been seen. It has to be said that such a film could only have been made in the last few years; the digital revolution has given film-makers tools that the pioneers of film in the 1900s could only ever dream of. Indeed, when Peter and I started making films these tools were still in the imagination of their creators and it was many years before the first fruits of their thinking were made available to the industry as a whole, and only then at a price most couldn't afford.

Today the situation is so different, brilliantly so, and in many ways it couldn't be a more exciting time to be involved in our type of film-making. The imagination is the only limit now to what can be put on the screen. There's no doubt there are films made that over-exploit the technology, but the best films are those with a strong story and wonderful characters, where the technology is used as a tool to enhance the story-telling. *The Pirates!* is certainly one of those and I hope that having seen it you will agree with me and be delighted to have been able to discover how the film was made and learn about the incredibly skilled crew who helped Peter put the whole thing together. Another wonderful story!

David Sproxton
Aardman

Afore Ye Go...
The Pirate Captain Speaks

To conclude this extraordinary saga of Pirates in an Adventure with Animators, we leave you with a hitherto unseen historical document that Mr Gideon Defoe found washed ashore in an empty grog bottle...

Hello, future-lubbers,

You probably think my piratical career is one gigantic non-stop thrill-ride of explosions and cutlass-waggling and dering-do. But I'll level with you — the nautical life has its fair share of dull days. Bobbing about a featureless ocean for months on end because your dodo ate the only working sextant. Eating bits of boiled jellyfish because the Albino Pirate forgot to pack any biscuits. Having to wait a hundred and fifty years for Scrabble to be invented. It can get you down. So to pass the time, me and the lads have devised a number of games. Our favourite game is seeing how many whelks we can fit in the Pirate with Gout's mouth. Our second favourite game is building statues of frisky-looking mermaids out of bits of old weevils. But our third-favourite game is sitting out on the deck, gazing up at the stars, wondering what the World of Tomorrow will bring.

Some of the less positive pirates predict that by 2012 you'll be living in a grim dystopia where emotions and puppies are banned, and people wear a lot of leather. Other not so imaginative pirates predict everything will be just like nowadays, only with fewer ruffles on your shirts and more tin foil covering the furniture.

Frankly, I have no clue what your bizarre era will be like. But one thing seems as inevitable as me finding barnacles in my belly button — at some point in the future a forward-thinking young writer with a nice haircut will decide to cash in on my celebrity and write a novel based on one of my adventures. That novel will no doubt be overlooked by a frankly blinkered literary establishment, but by good fortune it will fall into the hands of a daring theatrical impresario, the P. T. Barnum of his age, and he will decide to adapt this great work into a lavish play.

Of course, this being the future, said play won't be performed on a stage, it will probably be exhibited up and down the land on those new-fangled zoetrope devices. I'm guessing that our heroic zoetrope wrangler – who will certainly have some shiny, atomic-age name like Peter – will be regarded by many as a lunatic visionary for attempting such a thing. "It can't be done!" the people will cry. "For a start, where would you hope to find an actor who could do justice to the Pirate Captain's luxuriant beard?" And those people will have a point – for though they will scour the globe in search of an appropriately hirsute thespian, none will have a beard to match mine.

So, at that point, I'm guessing the lunatic visionary will decide that the only way to recreate me in all my hairy glory will be via the medium of puppets. Like a crazed Dr. Moreau he will carry out terrifying genetic experiments in order to concoct an entire army of strange, pale-skinned mole-people, which will be known as 'animators'. These godforsaken creatures will labour away for years in semi-darkness, moving the puppet versions of me inch by tortuous inch to give the illusion of life. It will be both horrifying and magnificent.

And when they are finally done, the finished production will be like nothing anybody has ever seen. I don't think I'm getting ahead of myself to suggest it will probably usher in a new age of global peace and prosperity, as warring nations and those from each side of the political spectrum put aside their differences, united in their admiration for what will be regarded as the Cultural Achievement of the Millennium. At the very least, I suspect they'll give away little figurines of me free with hamburgers.

Anyway, on the off-chance this all comes to pass exactly like I imagined, it seems likely there will be some sort of glossy 'making-of' book, which is why I'm writing this small contribution. In a minute, I will stick it in a bottle and cast it adrift in the ocean, in the hope it washes up on some distant shore and reaches your future selves. It is, I'll admit, a stupid way of delivering correspondence, but honestly – have you seen the cost of stamps these days? Ridiculous!

Hugs,

The Pirate Captain
Blood Island, 1838

The Pirates! Credits

ANIMATION SUPERVISOR
Loyd Price
SUPERVISING ART DIRECTOR
Matt Perry
VISUAL EFFECTS SUPERVISOR
Andrew Morley
HEAD OF STORY
Rejean Bourdages
PRODUCTION DESIGNER
Norman Garwood
DIRECTOR OF PHOTOGRAPHY
Frank Passingham
EDITED BY
Justin Krish
MUSIC BY
Theo Shapiro
SENIOR ANIMATION SUPERVISOR
Jay Grace
CO-DIRECTOR
Jeff Newitt
EXECUTIVE PRODUCER
Carla Shelley
PRODUCED BY
Julie Lockhart
Peter Lord
David Sproxton
BASED UPON A BOOK BY
Gideon Defoe
SCREENPLAY BY
Gideon Defoe
DIRECTED BY
Peter Lord

CAST
THE PIRATE CAPTAIN
Hugh Grant
THE PIRATE WITH A SCARF
Martin Freeman
QUEEN VICTORIA
Imelda Staunton
CHARLES DARWIN
David Tennant
BLACK BELLAMY
Jeremy Piven
CUTLASS LIZ
Salma Hayek
PEG LEG HASTINGS
Lenny Henry
THE PIRATE KING
Brian Blessed
THE ALBINO PIRATE
Russell Tovey
THE PIRATE WITH GOUT
Brendan Gleeson
THE SURPRISINGLY CURVACEOUS PIRATE
Ashley Jensen
THE PIRATE WHO LIKES SUNSETS AND KITTENS
Ben Whitehead
ADMIRAL COLLINGWOOD
Mike Cooper
SCARLETT MORGAN
David Schneider

ADDITIONAL VOICES
Tom Doggart
Sophie Jerrold
Sophie Laughton
Peter Lord
Kayvan Novak
David Schaal

CASTING
Kate Rhodes James
CHARACTER DESIGN
Jonny Duddle
Carlos Grangel
PUPPET DESIGN
Kate Anderson
Andrew Bloxham
Anne King
PRODUCTION MANAGER
Richard Beek
PRE PRODUCTION AND POST PRODUCTION MANAGER
Tara Knowles
HEAD OF MODEL-MAKING PRODUCTION
Lizzie Spivey
HEAD OF ART DEPARTMENT PRODUCTION
Zoe Starzak
VISUAL EFFECTS AND PRE-VISUALISATION PRODUCER
Benjamin Lock
HEAD OF CAMERA AND LIGHTING
Tom Barnes
CO-EXECUTIVE PRODUCER
Sarah Smith

ANIMATION
SENIOR LEAD ANIMATOR
Ian Whitlock
CHARACTER LEAD ANIMATORS
Will Becher
Suzy Parr
Christopher Sadler
KEY ANIMATORS
Dug Calder
Malcolm Lamont
Dan Ramsay
Claire Rolls
Andy Symanowski
Darren Thomson

ANIMATORS
Alison Evans
Jo Fenton
Julia Peguet
Christophe Peladan
Laurie Sitzia-Hammond
Andrew Spilsted
Lee Wilton
Ludovic Berardo
Jason Comley
Steve Cox
Todor Iliev
Gareth Love
Florian Perinelle
Philippe Tardif
Wendy Griffiths
Richard Haynes
Rhodri Lovett
Dean Watson
Darren Burgess
Jan-Erik Maas
Grant Maisey
Pascual Perez

2D ANIMATED SEQUENCES
Michael Schlingmann
ASSISTANT ANIMATORS
Rita Crespo Sampaio
Thomas Sewell
LIP SYNC ANIMATORS
Dani Abram
Shona De Bradney
Jordan Davies
Michael Green
Peg Serena
2D ASSISTANT ANIMATOR
Justine Waldie

STORY
ADDITIONAL STORY MATERIAL
Kevin Cecil
Andy Riley
SENIOR STORYBOARD ARTISTS
Michael Salter
David Vinicombe
Jean-Philippe Vine
STORYBOARD ARTISTS
Ashley Boddy
Jay Clark
Andy Janes
Paul Bolger
Matt Jones
Kris Pearn
Mike Smith
Sharon Smith
Rob Stevenhagen
Jean-Paul Vermeulen
Ian Matthews
ASSOCIATE PRODUCER
Sue Breen
PRODUCTION ASSISTANT
Victoria Evans

MODEL-MAKING
ADDITIONAL CHARACTER DESIGN
Christophe 'Zebe' Lourdelet
Jeff Newitt
Michael Salter
DESIGN SCULPTOR
Debbie Smith
SCULPTOR
Linda Langley
MODEL TEAM SUPERVISORS
Claire Cohen
Claire Drewett
Jim Parkyn
Harriet Thomas
Elinor Weston
ARMATURE SUPERVISOR
Jon Frier
FOAM SUPERVISOR
Andy Spradbery
PAINT SUPERVISOR
Ruth Mitchell
SENIOR MODEL-MAKERS
James Young
Jill Adams
Martin Adamson
Gideon Bohannon
Chris Brock
Sheila Clarkson
Andrew Gordon
Hanna Habermann
Will Harding
Diane Holness
Rob Horvath
Nigel Leach
Rebecca Levine
Cormac McKee
Gareth Northrop
Jemma Proctor
Kev Scillitoe
Catherine Slade
Jay Smart
Lisa Stevens
Nancy Stott
Lee Tetzner
Kevin Wright
SENIOR PAINTERS
Arlene Arrell
Steve Carey
Yvonne Fox
Nichola Howells
Anna Warsop
PAINTERS
George Cox
Anita Melia
Becky Redhead
Jim Taylor
Alex Williams
James Wilson
MODEL-MAKERS
Kate Berry
Deva Chellun
Suzanne Clarke
Sarah Fisher
Lois Garland
Katy Howarth
Tandie Langton
Jonathan Lendrum
Ian Matthews
Sarah Milburn
Sonia Iglesias-Rey
Henriette Tomczak
Andrew Trim
Katherine Archer
Amy Bridger
Robert Carr
Kerry Dyer
Gina Eversfield
Alex Howes
Michael Mullins
Frankey Pinnock
Ellen Seto
Megan Sinfield
Liz Smith
Richard Smith
Emily Stone
Joshua Stonehouse-Ashman
Joanne Symanowski
Cherie Taylor
Olga Duraj-Teordorczyk
Nicola Williams
Ashley Woodford
Kristy Wright

PRODUCTION MANAGER
Hilary Thorn
PRODUCTION CO-ORDINATOR
Caroline Hague
PRODUCTION ASSISTANTS
Gail Mallett
Kate Warburton
PUPPET AND MAINTENANCE CO-ORDINATOR
Caroline Hague
PUPPET WRANGLERS
Jake Gorton
Adele Lovett

RAPID PROTOTYPING
PRODUCTION MANAGER
Jacky Priddle
SUPERVISOR
Amanda Darby
TDs
Nathan Guttridge
Philip Child
CG FACIAL RIGGER
David Brooks
MODELLERS/RIGGERS
Mike Cole
Tanja Krampfert
PRODUCTION CO-ORDINATOR
Caroline Hamann
LIBRARIAN
Pip Whateley
PRODUCTION ASSISTANT
Kelly Barker

ART DEPARTMENT
ART DIRECTORS
Phil Lewis
Sarah Hauldren
Matt Sanders
GRAPHIC DESIGN SUPERVISOR
Gavin Lines
ASSISTANT ART DIRECTORS
Kitty Clay
Richard Edmunds
Manon Wright
CARPENTER AND WORKSHOP MANAGER
Cathryn Webber
SENIOR SET DRESSERS
Andy Brown
Sophie Brown
Lorna Cashmore
James Held
SET DRESSERS
Joe Bourbon
Paul Bryant
Stuart Mallaber
Laura Savage
Rosa Dodd
Simon Farrell
Kizie Gibson
Magadalena Osinska
Rob Slagter
HEAD OF PROPS
Jane Kite
SENIOR PROP MAKERS
David Howarth
Damian Neary
Karl Wardle
SPECIALIST PROP MAKER
Jack Slade
PROP MAKERS
Diego Soriano Gomez
Gary Roberts
Oliver Geen
Jemma Stidston
GLASS MAKER
Kim George
CONCEPTUAL ARTISTS
Adam Cootes
Bernhard Haux
Andrew Lavery
Marcin Lichowski
Gavin Lines
Alfred Llupia Perez
Norman Walshe
Darrell Warner
PRODUCTION CO-ORDINATOR
Stef Ingram
PRODUCTION ASSISTANT
Georgina Reynolds
MODEL RIGGING ANIMATION RIGGING SUPERVISOR
David Lawson
SENIOR ANIMATION RIGGERS
Alan Barrett
Alan Scrase
Simon Peeke
ANIMATION RIGGERS
Andree Neeman
Chris Gough
Cathy Northrup-Snelling

EDITORIAL
ASSOCIATE EDITORS
Angharad Owen
David McCormick
FIRST ASSISTANT EDITOR
Andrew Ward
ASSISTANT EDITORS
Tom Doggart
Eiko Emersleben
Gemma Lewis
Colin Bassett
Chris Gape
ASSISTANT VFX EDITOR
Judith Allen
Laurie Morgan
TRACK BREAKDOWN
Chris Stock

PRODUCTION
FIRST ASSISTANT DIRECTOR
Ben Barrowman
SECOND ASSISTANT DIRECTOR
Richard Bowen
THIRD ASSISTANT DIRECTOR
David Button
Samuel Horton
CONTINUITY
Sophie Smith
Rebecca Hall
PRODUCTION CO-ORDINATORS
Jo Miller
Sharron Traer
Claire Watson
PRODUCTION ASSISTANTS
Peter Evans
Richard Lake
Emma Bell
RUNNERS
Tom Wright
Robin Crowther-Smith
Alistair Mair
Heather Moore
Phillip Wrigley
PRODUCTION ACCOUNTANT
Karen Walter
ASSISTANT PRODUCTION ACCOUNTANTS
Yvonne Pfister
Matt Willis
FINANCE ASSISTANT
Angela Curtis
ASSISTANT TO MR LORD
Amy Wood

ASSISTANT TO MS LOCKHART
Emily Metcalfe

UNIT PUBLICISTS
Arthur Sheriff
Fumi Kitahara
Lucy Wendover

UNIT PHOTOGRAPHER
Luke Smith

CAMERA

SENIOR LIGHTING CAMERA
Dave Alex Riddett
Paul Smith

LIGHTING CAMERA
Charles Copping
Jeremy Hogg
Laura Howie

MOTION CONTROL OPERATORS
Willy Marshall
Linda Hamblyn
George Milburn
Chris Lovegrove
Jon Ryan
Mohan Sandhu

SENIOR CAMERA ASSISTANT
Churton Season

CAMERA ASSISTANTS
James Fisher
Beth MacDonald
John Quarrell
Ben Stradling
Ellie Brown
Hannah Gamlin
Tim Hogg
Chris Johnson
Jamie Kennerley
Molly King
Sam Morris

LIGHTING

GAFFER
Richard Hosken

ELECTRICIANS
Peter Marshall
Geoff Palmer
Clive Scott
Adam Vernon
Vinny Cannon
Eddie Armstrong
Joe Clevely
Peter Scott

TECHNICAL & PIPELINE

EQUIPMENT MANAGER
Luke Smith

DEVELOPMENT ENGINEER
Alan Gregory

MAINTENANCE ENGINEER
Robert Gregory

MECHANICAL ENGINEER
Morgan Roe

ELECTRONICS ENGINEER
Dave Roberts

SYSTEMS SUPPORT TECHNICAN
Toby Chilcott

LEAD PRODUCTION SOFTWARE DEVELOPER
Ian Wootten

PRODUCTION SOFTWARE DEVELOPER
Eugene Getov
Rick Hurst
Andrew McGregor

WIREMAN
Barry Haskins

TECHNICAL DEPARTMENT CO-ORDINATORS
Deena Mathews
Scott Metcalfe
Kate Munkenbeck-Stannard

PRE-VISUALISATION AND VISUAL EFFECTS

DIGITAL ART DIRECTOR
Alfred Llupia Perez

TDs
Javier Alonso
Peter Bailey
Tim Brade
Paul Burton
Giacomo Cavaletti
Alastair Dixon
William Earl
Mauro Frau
Grant Hewlett
Christian Jelen
Pierre Pages
Daniele Tagliaferri
Ben Thomas
Rupert Thorpe
Bradley Stilwell

CHARACTER TD
Martin Orlowski

FX SUPERVISOR
Rod McFall

DIGITAL FX ARTISTS
Andrei Allerborn
Stuart Armiger
Anders Hakansson
Michael Nixon
Cornelius Porzig
Farhan Qureshi
Alberto Della Regina
Chris Soyer

CG SUPERVISORS
Ted Chaplin
Chris King
Benjamin Toogood

CG MODELLERS AND RIGGERS
Helen Duckworth
Sergi Caballer Garcia
Ryan Harrington
Christopher Livesey
Tom Lord
Alex Parkin
Aleksandar Pavlovic
Nick White
Dean Wright

2D SUPERVISORS
Ben Pierre
Mike Shirra

DIGITAL MATTE PAINTING AND TEXTURE ARTISTS
Andrew Cunningham
James Furlong
Johan Gay
Diego Goberna

SENIOR SYSTEMS ENGINEER
Shane McEwan

SYSTEMS ADMINISTRATOR
Gerald Davies

RENDER WRANGLERS
Alexander Phoenix
Anya Scarpa
Thomas Stevenson
James Walker

PIPELINE AND TOOL DEVELOPMENT
Tom Downes
Spencer Drayton
Sarah MacDonald
Michael Scarpa
Robin Watson

DIGITAL ANIMATION SUPERVISOR
Lesley Headrick

PRE-VISUALISATION AND DIGITAL ANIMATORS
Jamie Bakewell
Olly Davis
Nick Hanks
Martin Haughey
Boris Hiestand
Dan Lane
Debbie Langford
Will Miller
Rebecca Rose

PRE-VISUALISATION DEVELOPMENT
Pawl Fulker

PRE-VISUALISATION TDs
Robert Nzengou-Tayo
Daniel Radley-Bennett

LEAD COMPOSITORS
Carl Chittenden
Robert Jackson
Howard Jones

DIGITAL COMPOSITORS
Robin Brown
George Deany
Giancarlo D'Erchie
Jesus Diez
Timur Khodzhaev
Nicha Kumkeaw
John McLaren
Andy Quinn
Ashwinsingh Rajput
Pablo Renedo
Owen Revell
Valeria Romano
Mykhailo Slavov
Fincher Trist
Tom Whittington
Kim Wiseman

VFX CO-ORDINATORS
Melanie Callaghan
Cara Davies
Dan Dixon
Amy James
Fifi Maree
Stuart Messinger
Jessica Newhouse-Smith
Tsvetomira Valcheva
Lindsay Weir

PRODUCTION ASSISTANTS
Paula Poveda-Urrutia
Melanie Thomas
Marcus Jose
Sian Campbell

POST PRODUCTION

POST PRODUCTION SUPERVISOR
Tom Barnes

SUPERVISING SOUND EDITOR
Adrian Rhodes

RE-RECORDING MIXERS
Andy Nelson
Mark Patterson

DIALOGUE EDITOR
Tim Hands

SOUND EFFECTS EDITORS
Nick Adams
Will Norie

SOUND EDITOR
Antony Bayman

DIALOGUE RECORDING MIXER
Nick Roberts

FOLEY ARTIST
Sue Harding

FOLEY MIXER
Paul Carr

ASSISTANT SOUND EFFECTS EDITOR
Julien Pirrie

DIGITAL RECORDIST
Robert Weatherall

ADR VOICE CASTING
Brendan Donnison

ADR RECORDING MIXER
Peter Gleaves
Re-Recording Studio
Goldcrest Post Production Ltd (London)

END TITLE DESIGN
Gavin Lines

DIGITAL INTERMEDIATE BY
Technicolor Creative Services

DIGITAL INTERMEDIATE COLOURIST
Max Horton

DIGITAL INTERMEDIATE PRODUCER
Begoña Lopez

DIGITAL INTERMEDIATE EDITORS
Jaime Leonard
Matt Watson

MUSIC

MUSIC EDITOR
Thomas Drescher

ORCHESTRATIONS
John Ashton Thomas
Tommy Laurence
Dave Metzger

MUSIC RECORDED AND MIXED BY
Chris Fogel

DIGITAL RECORDIST
Lewis Jones

MUSIC CONDUCTED BY
Gavin Greenaway
Auricle Operator
Chris Cozens

MUSIC RECORDED AND MIXED AT
Abbey Road Studios

SCORE SUPERVISORS
Becky Bentham
Catherine Grieves

MUSIC PREPARATION
Mark Graham

ORCHESTRA CONTRACTORS
Isobel Griffiths
Jo Buckley

CHOIR
London Voices

MUSIC CONSULTANT
Nick Angel

FOR AARDMAN ANIMATIONS

SENIOR MANAGEMENT
Sean Clarke
Kerry Lock
Paula Newport
Gareth Overton-Edwards
Steve Pegram

CREATIVE DEVELOPMENT
Alicia Gold
Paul Kewley

SYSTEMS ENGINEERING
Systems Manager
Pete Forde
Systems Administrators
Tudor Georgescu
Colin Mooney

PRODUCTION AND STUDIO INFRASTRUCTURE
Zena Allen
Ruth Burnett
Joanna Cave
Natalie Collier
Ian Fleming
Lew Gardiner
Fran Hawley
Kat Jane
Kim Jones
Joe Maxwell
Paul Reeves
Michelle Rogers
Nathan Sale
Vicky Sale
Andy Woodland

SENIOR TECHNICAL SUPPORT ENGINEER
John Morrissey

IT SUPERVISOR
Howard Arnault-Ham

IT
Adam Brown
Colin Coulter
Richard Crocombe
Jeremy Donovan
Mark Keightley
Luke Padfield
David Waters

FACILITIES MANAGEMENT
Stuart Briggs
Drew Colenso
Alistair Gue
Tony Prescott
Facilities Glenn Collins
James Filbin
Adrienn Kun
Fay Morgan
Ibrahima Ndiaye
Miguel Santa Cruz
Bob Shortman
Anne Webb

FOR SONY PICTURES ANIMATION

Ronni G Coulter
Matt Davis
Peter Jensen
Rebecca Kuska
Tammy Lee
Don Levy
Duke Logan
Pam Marsden
Olivier Mouroux
Dorothy C Rayburn

SET CONSTRUCTION
Cod Steaks

SENIOR PRODUCER
Susannah Lipscombe

PROJECT/CONSTRUCTION MANAGER
Mike Applebee

HEAD OF ENGINEERING
Paul Drake

HEAD OF PROPS
Louise Vergette

PROJECT CO-ORDINATOR
Renae Cronin

TEAM LEADERS
Paul Cowle
Matthew Healey

PROPS
Daniel Broadley
Duncan Miller
Jonny Parsons

SENIOR SET BUILD/MODEL-MAKERS
Justeen Bailey
Joan Caswell
Maddy Cole
Georgie Everard
Andrew Farago
Oliver Hayles
Patrick McGrath
John Pealing
Roger Tarry
Jamie Thomas
Abi Vickery

SET BUILD/MODEL-MAKERS
Tom Astley
Tom Bayliss
Mel Callum
Jamie Carruthers
Mike Drake
Jax Goodyear
Tony Hallam
Helen Javes
Paul Lynch
Ian Penny
Steve Priddle
Dawn Stewart-Tiller
Peter Williams
Thecla Kip-Mallinson

HEAD PAINTERS
Katie Hughes
Thecla Kip-Mallinson

PAINTERS
Pat Bailey
Ro Cohen
Celia Garrad
Keri-Lyn Sheppard

CNC TECHNICIAN
Will Mullins

WORKSHOP MANAGER
Trevor Butler

PRODUCTION MANAGER
Jutta Coulain

APM
Kim Jackson

PRODUCTION ASSISTANTS
Jan Bujak
Rebecca Jackson
Joe Noble

PRODUCTION ARMATURES AND SPECIALIST PROPS
John Wright Modelmaking
Joel Calver
Ann Evans
Kenny Monger
Ed Sams
Dave Weaver
John Wright

ADDITIONAL VISUAL EFFECTS
Double Negative

SUPERVISOR
Jody Johnson

EXECUTIVE PRODUCER
Melissa Taylor

PRODUCER
Clare Tinsley

LINE PRODUCER
Darryl Li

CO-ORDINATORS
Sanchari Chowdhury
Cindy Khoo
Emma Moffat

2D SUPERVISOR
Oliver Atherton
Peter Jopling
Ian Simpson

3D SUPERVISOR
Rick Leary
David Vickery

EDITORIAL
Benjamin Chua
XinYi Phua
Bobby Sass

2D ARTISTS
Michael Allen
Amirah Busairi
Agustin Cavalieri
Saptarshi Chakraborty
Eric Chan
ShuYin Chan
KaiHsin Chin
Kunal Chindakar
Christopher Crowel
Michaela Danby
Raji Kodja
Jeffrey Koh
Jessica Kong
Chris Lee
Sky Lim
Young Lim
Roy Tay
Jacky Toh

3D ARTISTS
Cori Chan
Dominic Drane
Leah Low
ShiHua Ng
Rokas Rakauskas
Sonny Sy
Alex Tan

ADDITIONAL VISUAL EFFECTS
Method Studios

EXECUTIVE PRODUCER
Drew Jones

VFX PRODUCER
Melody Woodford

2D SUPERVISOR
Sean Danischevsky

PRODUCTION COORDINATOR
Daniel Matley

COMPOSITORS
Antony Allen
Paul Daiko
Paula Olszowska
Andrew Pinson
Joanna Wand

JUNIOR COMPOSITORS
Giorgia Pulvirenti
Marek Solowiej
Jenny Wan

WITH THANKS TO
Pete Baynham
Mark Burton
Jim Campbell
Jemaine Clement
Martin Clunes
David Cox
Martin Elliott
Doug Ikeler
Uli Meyer
Stephen Moore
Rich Murkin
Prakash Patel
Nick Park
Steve Price
Kisaburo Toriumi
Sara Woodhatch
The Royal Society

NO DODOS WERE MADE EXTINCT DURING THE MAKING OF THIS MOTION PICTURE

Acknowledgements

AVAST AND BELAY, there! Not many authors will tell you this, but anyone can write a book – just so long as you can get enough people to help you do it! And this is where I get to thank the people who helped . . .

I'll begin with the talented people – writers, designers, model-makers, animators, technicians, musicians and voice talents – without whom there would not have been a film to write about; and, in particular (and in alphabetical order) those who shared their experiences of bringing the world of *The Pirates!* to life: Kate Anderson, Tom Barnes, Will Becher, Richard Beek, Brian Blessed, Andrew Bloxham, Rejean Bourdages, Ted Chaplin, Gideon Defoe, Jonny Duddle, Martin Freeman, Norman Garwood, Jay Grace, Hugh Grant, Ashley Jensen, Justin Krish, Gavin Lines, Julie Lockhart, Peter Lord, Michael Lynton, Hannah Minghella, Andrew Morley, Jeff Newitt, Bob Osher, Julia Peguet, Suzy Parr, Frank Passingham, Alfred Llupia Perez, Matt Perry, Loyd Price, Jacky Priddle, Adrian Rhodes, Christopher Sadler, Theodore Shapiro, Laurie Sitzia-Hammond, Dave Sproxton, Imelda Staunton, David Tennant, Russell Tovey, Ian Whitlock and Lee Wilton.

Also, special thanks to Jess Houston and Helen Neno.

Then there are the folk at Bloomsbury who helped the story behind the filming of *The Pirates!* become a book: Rebecca McNally, Publishing Director, and Val Brathwaite, Creative Director, for being Aardman visionaries; Rachel Moss, who did much initial work on the project, including conducting many of the interviews; copy-editor Rosalind Turner, who trimmed and tidied up my prose before it went out into the world; Mandy Archer, my ceaselessly patient, accommodating and inspiring editor; and designer Nick Avery, who is responsible for giving the book such an adventurously swashbuckling look!

Lastly, as always, for their support and encouragement: my agent Philip Patterson of Marjacq Scripts and my long-suffering partner, David Weeks.

It is twenty years since I began association with Aardman Animations and I am proud to be involved with another of their projects – especially one that is, without question, their most spectacularly ambitious film.

I thank'ee, me hearties!

Brian Sibley